IDAHO LORE

Gathering
of Nuggets

Idaho Lore

Prepared by the Federal Writers' Project of the
Work Projects Administration *Idaho*

VARDIS FISHER, STATE DIRECTOR

AMERICAN GUIDE SERIES

398.2
731

The CAXTON PRINTERS, Ltd.
Caldwell, Idaho
1939

FEDERAL WORKS AGENCY

WORKS PROGRESS ADMINISTRATION

F. C. HARRINGTON, Commissioner
FLORENCE KERR, Assistant Commissioner
HENRY G. ALSBERG, Director of the
Federal Writers' Project

Printed, lithographed, and bound in the United States of America by
The CAXTON PRINTERS, Ltd.
Caldwell, Idaho
52343
First printing December, 1939

TABLE OF CONTENTS

◦☙◦

469215

LIST OF ILLUSTRATIONS

INTRODUCTION

❧

THIS is not a Sunday school text nor a collection of smoke-house and horror stories. It is simply a batch of yarns and experiences of the early days garnered from a variety of sources. If not all of it is honest-to-goodness folklore, that is because the compilers were interested in good stories rather than in fine distinctions, and because the job of gathering folklore is one for a trained specialist. Some of this volume is folklore and some of it is only lore; but all of it is significantly pertinent, we believe, to Idaho's past.

Among members of the Project staff, the book owes most to Mrs. Violet Eggers for her indefatigable industry in the field and to William Runyan for his drawings. A list of all the volunteers who assisted us would fill several pages. Acknowledgment is due the departments of English and history in the State's universities and colleges and many of its high schools; and to more than a thousand contributors, ranging from the Governor to old-timers who live out in the mountains far from the end of the road. To all of them we give our thanks for drawing so willingly on their memories to make this book possible.

We are also indebted to Adrian Troy, of the Federal Art Project of Chicago, for the linoleum cuts.

Idaho Lore is the first state collection in the folklore series of the Federal Writers' Project, edited by B. A. Botkin, national folklore editor.

VARDIS FISHER

Tales

PART I—TALES

THE TALES included in this section, chosen from hundreds, are of several kinds. Under Quasi-Historical are chronicled events which, there seems no good reason to doubt, actually happened, though in many or in all particulars the truth doubtless varied from that which is given here. In any case, these are not legends except in the ways by which oral transmission has edited and added to them. Such are the anecdotes of "Idaho Joke Book," a collection of amazing incidents that savor of the tall tale; and though the reader may use all the salt he wishes, he is asked to remember that for every one of these there is an Idahoan alive today, and often several, to solemnly swear that the events are not here exaggerated in the telling. The skeptic will suspect at least that a few of them belong to the lore of the world, transplanted here and established by lively imagination as facts. Out of deference to their witnesses, do not call them tall tales: those who authenticate them would "wax wrothful" if these stories were debased to the level of a liar's fertile fancy. Nor are all those under Tall and Broad the sort of thing that emanates from a liars' contest. Some of them are tall tales, but most of the tall tales submitted (and rejected) seemed to strive only for the kind of preposterous exaggeration that makes a ski out of a locust leaf and a thunderstorm out of a hiccough. As a matter of fact, the tall tales commonest in every part of the State and most frequently repeated are almost invariably pointless and childish. Parenthetically, it seems strange that so few hillbilly raconteurs perceive the comical and often devastating effect of understatement. On the contrary, they vie with one another in the whopping lie and exhaust themselves by piling inept exaggeration until the result is the sudden collapse of the story under its inflation.

In the Tall and Broad section, as well possibly as in others, the reader will now and again be fetched up by an old chestnut. Someone has said that the only new thing in the world is what we have forgotten; and if the memories of some readers are unconscionably long, they are asked not to forget that every story, at least in variants, reaches back to Adam. When one person declared that one of the stories in this book was familiar to him as a babe in Michigan, the story was given to another. He slapped his thighs and yowled with delight. This experiment was repeated until it became clear that one man's joy was another man's pain; and that if every story was to be discarded because it had been a commonplace to infants in Michigan, there wouldn't be any book left.

Gathering Indian legends is a task for the ethnologist. Those included here are present chiefly because of their sentimental value for Idahoans and not because it is assumed that they are a contribution to their field.

QUASI·HISTORICAL

When Smallpox Was Terror

In 1862 there lived at Fort Boise a major, his wife, and five children, one of whom became unaccountably droopy. When the child seemed to be getting worse, the major called a doctor who took one long stare around him and headed for the door. He shouted that it was smallpox and vanished. After the child died nobody wanted to bury it; but after a grave was dug, the father wrapped the child in a blanket and laid it outside the cabin, and some soldiers roped it from a distance, not venturing within thirty feet of it, and dragged it to the grave and tumbled it in. The mother died next, and one by one the other children followed her; and the appalled father laid them outside and they were roped and dragged away. When the major felt himself stricken, he wrapped a blanket around him and lay close by the door to die. After he was buried, the cabin was destroyed by fire. These seven graves are still marked in the old burying grounds near the site of the fort.

A Practical Chinese

China Charlie was called upon to make a coffin for a dead Chinese. Without bothering to measure the corpse, he went ahead, and discovered after his labor was done that the coffin was by several inches too short; so Charlie took a meat saw and was busy sawing the legs off at the knees when he was overwhelmed by a score of jabbering Chinese. Charlie compromised by knocking an end off the coffin and slipping a tea box over it.

An Impractical Joke

In early days when Pocatello was nothing much except the Q. P. (Quiet Place) Saloon, a man by the name of Miller was everlastingly bragging of what he would do with stick-up men if any of them ever accosted him; whereupon, weary of his chin music, several fellows overtook him one night on

The Plague

his way home and held him up. They took from him his watch and seventy-five dollars; and a few minutes later, Miller was back at the saloon, declaring that robbers had assaulted him and he had slain five. When, the following day, he received a C. O. D. parcel that cost him ten dollars, and opened it to discover his watch and money, he was as crestfallen as any braggart could be.

But he got his revenge. Suspecting who the perpetrators were, and seeing them board the train one day for Salt Lake City to attend a convention, he wired ahead to the police, asking them to arrest at the station upon arrival a dangerous gang of rascals who had been terrorizing Pocatello. Miller went on the same train to watch the fun; but when the patrol wagon came up and policemen saw this stranger laughing until tears washed down his cheeks, they decided that he was either drunk or crazy and took him along also. All day long the arrested men, who were among the social and business leaders of Pocatello, raved and swore in their cells, but the policemen wouldn't believe a word they said. It was not until a lodge brother found and identified them that the police realized their terrific blunder and set the indignant fellows free. The story does not say what happened to Miller.

Deadshot Reed

Deadshot Reed was for many years one of the most picturesque and undecipherable persons in Idaho. He lived in the primitive wilderness close by the Middle Fork of Salmon River; and how many men he killed nobody ever knew. He admitted wearily that he did not know himself. Nor did he seem to know how many children he had. When asked one day, he scratched his head and looked around him. "Wal," he said, "I think I got a kid for ever' dog on the place and I reckon I got about eleven dogs."

Death of the Juggernaut

When a flour mill was established at Fort Hall, the Indians were both curious and alarmed. They gathered by scores and tried to decide whether or not the white man running the mill was a god. Unable to settle the matter, a gang of them sneaked into the mill late one night and switched on the power; and in the excitement that followed, an Indian was killed. Thereupon, the redskins decided that the outfit was run by an evil spirit and came to it the next day. While some kept the miller busy, others slipped behind the mill and set it afire. The miller and his family lived in quarters in the rear of the mill. In the sudden and overwhelming fire, they were all burned to death.

Hundred Dollar Jim

Unusual among the characters of southern Idaho was Hundred Dollar Jim, an old prospector who for many years lived in the Hailey area. Neither the man's name nor the location of his mine was known. Periodically he came to town and stopped at the general store to buy supplies, and at the Northern Star Casino where he always placed a hundred dollars in gold dust on a number of the roulette wheel. Win or lose, he never wagered twice in the same day. One December, when the snow was deep, it was remembered that Jim had not come to town and a searching party set out to find him and his treasure. They went up Warm Springs Creek; and after they had gone a few miles they saw Jim across from them on a mountain flank, drawing a laden sled through the snow. A few minutes later, a thaw loosened the deep snow into a slide and they saw Jim carried downward and buried. So far as is known, he was pitched into Dollar Lake, a very deep body of water, and both Jim and his treasure are still there.

Indian Punishment of Adultery[1]

The chiefs of the Nez Perce, five in number, were sitting in council as a tribunal last week to investigate charges against members of the tribe, male and female. The most important case was that of an unfaithful spouse and her seducer. Upon hearing the evidence pro and con, it was decided that the parties were guilty. The "gay Lothario" was sentenced to receive twenty lashes and to be mulcted to the amount of three cows and two cayuses. The "dusky Dulcinea" suffered a flagellation for her part of the guilt; her former lord and master could reclaim her if he so desired.

---

1 Lewiston *Age*, Dec. 3, 1864.

*Indian Punishment
of Adultery*

The Dewey-Koenig Shooting

Bill Dewey, famous early Idahoan and builder of both Dewey and Silver City, had a close friend named Summercamp, who, upon his arrival from Germany, set up a saloon, with a brewery in the basement. He financed operations on the Black Jack mine of Florida Mountain and was to share in the earnings if the mine proved successful. He told Dewey when he wanted to drink to go behind the bar and help himself; but the barkeeper, a man named Koenig, did not like the trespassing. For a time he said nothing; but later, losing his temper, he asked Dewey what he was doing behind the bar. Dewey said he had Summercamp's permission, and there for several days the matter rested.

But Koenig couldn't get it off his mind; and one day, getting drunk, he swore that he would kill Dewey if the man bothered him again. A week later he became suddenly friendly and invited Dewey to the basement with him to taste of the new brew. On their way they went through the dark and windowless maltroom; and there, while Dewey was framed by the light of the doorway, Koenig drew a gun and fired. Dewey retreated, firing as he went but unable to see his foe; and it was not until later that he learned he had dropped Koenig with his first shot.

The Story of Bruneau John[1]

Bruneau John was one of the most interesting characters of the bloody Bannack War of 1878, the record of which forms one of the darkest blotches on the pages of Idaho history. John was a member of the Bannack tribe but during the memorable contest he left the campfires of his fathers and arrayed himself on the side of the whites to exterminate those who waged war. It was his Paul Revere ride to save the settlers of Bruneau Valley that won for him fame and made his name a household word in many an Idaho home.

The Bannack uprising was not unexpected in some parts of the State, but, strange to relate, where the Indians were best known, where they had daily met white people and traded their skins and game for food, the people scouted the idea of their dusky "friends" going on the warpath. They could not bring themselves to believe these Indians, many of

---

1 By permission of the Nampa *Free Press*.

Indian Raid

whom they had frequently befriended and most of whom were exceedingly mild mannered, would ever dream of massacre, and when Bruneau John some time before the redskins went on the trail, which they blazed with skeletons and the embers of ruined homes, told them there was imminent danger of an outbreak, they laughed at him and assigned to imagination his solemn words of warning.

For the most part, the people living about the old-time haunts of the Indians made no preparations to resist attack, and when the savages donned their war paint and went forth to kill and plunder and burn, these whites found themselves in a position of pitiful helplessness.

The first blood was shed by the Bannacks on the Snake River, near the mouth of the Bruneau. Their plan was to swoop down upon the settlers of Bruneau and kill them all. When they reached Snake River, the Indians found a large freight outfit, which they proceeded to plunder, butchering the freighters in a most diabolical manner. It was here that John Bascombe and James Ferguson fell after a brilliant fight against overwhelming odds. Their bodies and those of the other freighters were revoltingly mutilated and left to rot in the sagebrush.

After the savages had reveled in the blood of their victims until their minds had become thoroughly inflamed, they attacked the contents of the wagons, gleefully scattering the articles about as a prelude to the bloody work ahead. An air of fiendish festivity reigned.

Bruneau John said that that night after the freighters had been killed immense bonfires were lighted, the flames darting high into the air illuminating, spectre-like, the surroundings.

About the edge of the circle lay the bodies of the freighters, ghastly relics of the day's terrible work. As a party of the Indians, about three hundred strong, went through the wagons throwing out the boxes and bursting them open, flinging about the contents in their wild recklessness, the remainder of the reds circled about in a weird war dance, chanting their uncanny death song, some of them darting out occasionally to plunge knives into the bodies of the freighters or deal crushing blows on their skulls with tomahawks, emitting unearthly yells of triumph as their ghoulish work proceeded. Finally, exhausted from their vigorous dancing, they turned in and were soon asleep.

So confident were they that their deviltry was not known that they did not take precaution to post sentries. Wrapped in their blankets, all but Bruneau John slept soundly. While not an active participant in the orgies, owing to a pretended injured leg, he uttered no word of remonstrance, realizing his life would pay the forfeit of such rashness. But the information that the redskins intended to massacre the people of the Bruneau Valley filled his soul with horror, and his mind was filled with schemes to save these friends who a short time before had turned a deaf ear to his warnings. All night he tossed about, feverishly endeavoring to evolve a plan to get the news to them.

Several times he had started to escape from the camp, but each time the barking of dogs aroused some of the other Indians and he was forced to retire again with the excuse that he had gotten up to relieve the pain in his leg. So when morning dawned he had found no way to give warning to the innocent settlers above whose heads was suspended worse than Damocles' sword.

As soon as the Indians had satisfied their hunger in the morning they renewed their work of plundering the contents of the wagons and to their great joy they discovered several large bottles of alcohol consigned to the firm of Danskin Brothers, of Boise. They were soon engaged in mixing a brew which they drank ravenously. Bruneau John encouraged this in the belief that he might slip away if his dusky brethren could be induced to drink to excess. The Indians became wildly hilarious, and Bruneau John described their antics as both ludicrous and terrible. Some of the young bucks, exuberant from the effects of the liquor, mounted their horses and catching the ends of the bolts of cloth, started the animals on a dead run, spreading the bright calicoes and spotless muslin in a wavy profusion over the tops of the sagebrush. This form of sport was indulged in until all the cloth was exhausted and the plains in the vicinity assumed a kaleidoscopic appearance. The drinking was continued until the entire party was maudlin. Paralyzed by the strong stimulant, one after another they rolled over on the ground intoxicated, and evening found nearly the entire party lying around like logs, those not absolutely prostrated being sufficiently dazed to be harmless. Bruneau John said that three men at that time could have killed the entire party.

As soon as the shades of evening fell, John slipped away from the camp and besotted devils and, mounting his horse, sped away to the Bruneau Valley to give the alarm. He rode the entire night, waking the people at every farmhouse and apprising them of their danger, and this time his tocsin was heeded. The people fled from their homes in haste, terror adding alacrity to their movements, and morning found every farm in the valley deserted and the frightened people fleeing to a neighboring valley where they congregated and prepared to resist the advance of the Bannacks.

The evening following Bruneau John's departure from the Snake River camp the Indians recovered from the effects of their debauch and started for the Bruneau Valley to carry out their plan of death and desolation. But they found the homes deserted and gave evidence of their disappointment by burning everything in their path. Scouts reported the assemblage of farmers in the adjoining valley, but the redskins decided not to attack them, pressing forward to South Mountain, killing and burning wherever opportunity presented itself. At South Mountain the Indians were forced into an engagement with the volunteers, and it was there they lost their chief, Buffalo Horn.

Bruneau John accepted a position as scout for the whites and served faithfully through the entire war. The War Department recognized his splendid services by presenting him with a silver medal which he proudly exhibited.

Frontier Entertainment

In the early days when Pocatello was only the Union Pacific Hotel, a trader's store, and the Q. P. Saloon, the barber shop was run by a negro named Williams. He had a very attractive wife who did housework around the village, and was accosted by so many ardent white gentlemen that the husband, waking one day to fury, took her to the edge of town and cut her throat. At about the same time, a man named Phelps murdered a sheepherder at Lava; and he and Williams were lodged in the same cell in the Blackfoot jail.

One day, while the sheriff was taking his afternoon nap, the two murderers picked the lock and escaped. Phelps was overtaken at Brigham City, Utah. Unwilling to take any more chances, the authorities decided to hang him at once and to make a celebration of the hanging. In consequence, invitations were printed and sent far and wide, and many persons came to see the luckless fellow tighten the rope. Williams a little later was caught in Montana. For his hanging, the same invitations were sent, with only the date changed.

A Murderer's Last Words

Michael Dunn in 1866 was convicted of murder in the first degree. When asked if he had any reason why judgment should not be passed, he said: "I killed McKay and the circumstances connected with it lie between myself and my God. I am not responsible to this tribunal. It is a case between me and God, and to Him alone am I responsible."

End of a Bully

In 1886, Bill Snyder was the bully of Boomerang, the name of the first village on the present site of Payette. Bill stood six feet three in his bare feet and weighed two hundred and twenty pounds. He was a mean hombre when

Frontier Entertainment

drunk; everyone in the town was afraid of him. One day, after beating his wife, he went to the brewery and bloated himself with drink, saying he was going to leave this settlement and go elsewhere to live. He said he was going to take his little black-and-tan dog, Dexter, with him, and he set out for the dog; but he never got there. Someone, hiding behind a tree, fired a shotgun loaded with slugs from a piece of bar lead. The charge blew a hole in Bill's side as big as a pancake. His wife came to his funeral with a black eye and a huge bruise on one of her cheeks.

The Widow with the Shiner.

The Life and Death of Joe Skeleton

Few men have suffered more and survived to tell of it than Joseph Skeleton, Lemhi pioneer. In the year of 1876, he was an ox-team freighter. One day, arriving at the Hawley place, he and the owner went to the corrals where Joe expected to choose some steers. While he was chasing the beasts, one of them attacked and shoved a horn through his throat. It severed his windpipe and came out under his right eye, tearing his face so badly that the flesh of one side could be lifted and laid back over on the other cheek. Nevertheless, Skeleton got up and walked away.

A doctor was summoned and a wagon, but Joe refused to be carried. Breathing with a horrible gurgling noise and bleeding like a stuck hog, he walked to the wagon and rode to town. He lived; but he had to be fed through a tube in his throat, and he lost his power of speech. Just the same, he continued as a freighter, now using as his lead animal a fresh cow so that he would always have milk. It is said that the terrible experience daunted him only once. Upon arriving in town and looking in a mirror he signaled that he wanted a gun.

He lived to survive other misfortunes, including the loss of a finger and a dislocated hip. The out-of-doors had no power to kill him: he died of influenza in bed in a house.

Blackfeet Justice[1]

Many snows ago, Blackfeet Indians camped east of a mountain and the Crows south. While the Blackfeet braves were out hunting, their squaws at a spring were surprised by Crow warriors who tortured and murdered all but one, who was unusually attractive. When the hunters returned, they found the butchered women, as well as footprints which showed that one had been taken captive. They knew by her moccasin print who she was.

They sent her husband, a cousin, and five brothers to rescue her. Upon coming within view of the Crow camp, it was decided that the husband should hide in the willows by a creek and wait until his wife came for water. When she came, he made his presence known and called softly, telling her to come at once. It should have been clear to him then that she was reluctant; for she said she would go to camp for a few of her things and return. In spite of her husband's arguments and protests, she went.

When she entered the camp she behaved strangely. She seemed dazed or in a dream, and the Indians gathered around to marvel at her conduct. The Crow chief who had taken her as a wife asked her what the trouble was. She replied, "The sun says go to the top of yonder hill where you will find six men. Kill them and bring me their scalps. Then go to the willows by the pool. You will find a strange man there: bring him alive to me."

The warriors obeyed, murdering and scalping the six braves and bringing the husband to his wife. The husband spoke to his wife when he came before her. Unable to understand the Blackfeet language, the Crows asked her what he said; and she replied: "He says, 'You smoke the pipe of the kinnikinnick and after the coals are red-hot, pour them on my bare chest.'" The Crows obeyed. Enduring

1 Based on material supplied by Medicine Eagle, a Blackfoot Indian.

without a murmur the terrible pain, the man said to his wife: "You are a heartless woman!"

"What," they asked, "did he say now?" "He says heat water to a boiling point and pour on his head and chest." This likewise was done; and out of intolerable agony the husband again reproached his wife. "He says to build for him a cross and hang him there and move camp immediately." Not knowing that this warrior was her husband, and thinking he wished punishment in atonement for some sin, the Crow braves hanged him to a tree.

But all the while, an old wrinkled squaw who understood the language had been quietly listening. She knew that the woman did not want to return to her own people. Rising, she sent her dog into hiding; and when camp was moved, she complained that she could not find her dog and would have to be left behind. As soon as the camp vanished she ran to the hanged man and cut the thongs that bound him, gave him moccasins and pemmican, and told him to be on his way.

Many moons again passed. When he was well, he called the braves around him and told them and the father of the woman what she had done. The warriors set out at once to find the Crows; and upon discovering the camp they surrounded it and captured every person within it. Drawing a knife, the father of the traitor cut off her left breast; whereupon he gave the knife to her mother who, weeping bitterly, cut off the right breast. The warriors then tossed the agonized woman across the flames of a big fire, those on either side catching her and tossing her back; until she sank exhausted and was burned alive.

The Killing of Bigfoot[1]

Starr Wilkinson, half of him white and the other half Cherokee Indian and Negro, was commonly believed before his death to be all Indian, and the most terrible monster who roamed southern Idaho during his time. Even though legend has doubtless exaggerated his size, given to him feet seventeen inches long, a chest as big as a barrel, and a speed afoot almost equal to that of a horse, it is known that he was an enormous man with feet so large that their imprint be-

---

[1] J. W. Wheeler was a few months later convicted for his alleged part in a stage robbery in the Blue Mountains in Oregon and sentenced to ten years. When freed in 1877, he went to California, where he committed suicide.

trayed him everywhere he went. It is said that three men once set out on fast horses to run him down and pursued him for thirty miles in one day and could not overtake him. But many a tale is told of him; and many are the versions of his death. This one is based on the story of an anonymous man who is said to have witnessed it.

Bigfoot's favorite field of slaughter lay between Boise and Silver City, and especially in a narrow defile a few miles south of Snake River. Here with his band of rascals he waited and one by one picked off the early settlers traveling between the two towns. He was a terror and a scourge; but he was also a most cunning villain who outwitted all attempts to capture him. In July of 1868 he met his man.

This was during the time of the Golden Chariot feud and the Marion More tragedy, when Silver City was in an uproar. Governor Ballard was beside himself with woes, and blackguards swarmed down the landscape. Among the respectable citizens was a tall young man of slight build, with dark brown hair, a smooth boyish face, and direct gray eyes. His name was J. W. Wheeler. He was a jolly merrymaker who gave gusto to any crowd in which he found himself; and he was, rumor declared, a dead shot.

The anonymous person (let us call him John Blank) was traveling from Silver City to Boise with a two-horse wagon when, feeling need of rest, he turned his horses free to graze and lay back to sun himself. He did not know he was near the narrow defile which Bigfoot used as an ambush. He did know something was not as it should be when he learned that his horses had been frightened and had run away. John set out to track them and was going down Reynolds Creek when, upon looking across a canyon, he saw three Indians coming toward him at full speed. The sight paralyzed him. It was not so much the sight of three Indians as it was of the incredible giant who raced ahead of the other two. Not knowing whether he had been seen, John dropped behind a shelf of rocks and waited, supposing that he would be scalped within a few minutes. In less than a minute, Bigfoot came thundering past like a buffalo bull, but he did not halt or look to right or left. He was headed for the road; and when John turned to gaze that way, he saw the stage coming in sight.

John had been paralyzed before, but now his blood was frozen when he heard the crack of a rifle and saw the second

of the racing Indians drop dead only twenty yards from him.
At the roar of the gun, Bigfoot vanished behind a rock, and
the third Indian turned in his tracks and skinned out of
sight with the speed of an antelope. The stage was still
coming. Charley Barnes, the driver, laid the whip to his
horses upon approaching the canyon, knowing it was
Bigfoot's hideout; but he did not know that the terrible
warrior was hiding behind a rock only a hundred yards away.
Nor did he learn it this day. He laid the whip on and sped
through the canyon and out of sight.

Bigfoot, visible to John, was now maneuvering in an
attempt to discover where his enemy was. He crawled to one
side of his huge rock and peered out, and then crawled to
the other; and when no one shot at him, he grew bolder.
After putting his ear to the ground and hearing nothing, he
tied a huge armful of sagebrush on his back and fell to his
hands and knees, intending to crawl away disguised. To
John's horror, the monster started in his direction; and
John's blood that had been thawed a little now turned to ice
again, and his hair rose like a thicket of grass. He was
staring fascinated at the enormous villain creeping toward
him when he was electrified by a clear voice that rang like
a bell. "Get up from there, Bigfoot, you old feather-headed
and leather-bellied coward!"

Bigfoot lost no time in getting up. As he rose, the voice
spoke again. "I can see you crawling off like a snake. But
this time you don't get any woman's scalp. Come and get
mine, you black-headed monster!" On his feet now, Bigfoot
perceived that the voice was coming from someone hidden in
a clump of willows. He leveled his long-barreled rifle at the
willows and said: "You coward, me no coward! You come
out and me scalp you, too!" At that, Wheeler sprang from
his hiding place and stood in full view, crying, "Here we are,
sail in!" The two men fired at almost the same instant.
Bigfoot staggered, but recovered and fired again, and then
hurled his gun down and went on a run toward the dead
Indian. After a few yards another shot staggered and spun
him, but he reached the dead man and seized his gun. He
fired a third time at the moment when Wheeler sent another
bullet into his huge frame. Bigfoot now staggered and
almost fell; but he kept his feet, and drew his knife with a
shout that raised John's hair until it looked like a roach of a
porcupine. With his knife ready, the giant went at his best

speed for Wheeler, who struck him with a fourth ball, and then with a fifth.

Without moving from where he stood, and with extraordinary coolness, Wheeler kept firing as the great fellow raced toward him. When thirty yards away, Bigfoot went down with a broken leg, never to rise again. Still without moving, Wheeler emptied the remainder of the shots into the prone body; whereupon he reloaded his gun and called: "How you like the way I shoot, old hoss? I'll bet you don't scalp any more white men in this canyon!" Bigfoot cried out not to shoot again, for he was dying; and Wheeler drew a revolver and went over to look at his fallen foe. Then he turned to John and shouted: "Come on down, whoever you are! There's no danger now." There was no danger now. Bigfoot was bleeding from twelve wounds, and had both legs and one arm broken. He asked for water, but Wheeler said: "Wait till I break your other arm." Wheeler fired and the good arm fell.

Then Wheeler went to a creek and fetched a canteen of water to the dying man's mouth, and Bigfoot drank all of it. He asked for whisky. Wheeler said he had a small bottle of whisky and ammonia which he carried for snakebites; and a pint of this Bigfoot gulped. Then he cried, "I'm sick and blind!" and fell back, apparently dead. But he was not dead. After a few minutes he revived and said he felt better; and asked to have the dust and paint washed from his face, so that the two men could see how handsome he was. And he was handsome, John reported later: it was a fine strong face with perfect teeth, but the black eyes were hard and wicked. He now said he had a last request to make: he did not want to be scalped or taken to Boise. He wanted to be dragged among the willows and buried under stones, with his gun at his side. Wheeler promised to do all this, and to break the gun so it could not be used again, if Bigfoot would tell who he was and where he had come from.

According to John's report, Bigfoot now told his story: that his father was a white man, Archer Wilkinson, who had been hanged for murder; that his mother was part Cherokee, part Negro. He himself had been named Starr for Thomas Starr, a desperado. In the Cherokee Nation he had loved a girl, but in an emigrant train en route to the West, she fell in love with an artist, whereupon Bigfoot choked the man to death and threw him into Snake River. He named the persons whom he had murdered. And then he died. It is said his death long remained a mystery because of Wheeler's promise not to reveal it.

The Skull Behind the Bar

In the days when the vigilantes disciplined with a rope, there lived a man in Dodge City, Kansas, named Bender. He had a daughter, a tall, bow-legged and gawky creature with a cast in one eye. They ran a roadhouse in Dodge City and murdered for profit—but not without carefully choosing their victims. They wanted men who had money, who were gullible, and who could not resist a bow-legged girl who danced with her hips. In the rear of the place they had a dark room from which men never emerged dead or alive.

They prospered. They prospered until a foolhardy sheriff decided to learn what happened to the men who entered that dark room; and after pretending to get himself groggy with whisky and amorous notions, he allowed the cockeyed wench to lure him into the darkness. Just what happened then, nobody will ever know. Bender was the only person who could have told, but long before morning he was out of Dodge City and on his way westward.

On the next day, there was no sign of life in the Bender saloon. Curious citizens resolved to investigate—and found

The Sheriff and the Cockeyed Siren.

The Skull
Behind the Bar

469215

much more than they wanted to see. They found the sheriff dead on the floor, with his head almost severed by a hatchet; and the girl dead at his side, with a hole through her off-color eye. She was clutching the hatchet. Half-buried, half-floating in a cistern under the floor were eight partially decomposed bodies, each with a crushed skull. And now the scene changes.

On the lonely road between Challis and Salmon in Idaho, a miner was riding a nag and leading a pack animal behind him when the laden beast, driven frantic by bloodsucking flies, dashed off, kicking and maddened, and disappeared. The next morning the miner found him on a grassy mountain meadow; but he found more than that. He found a fearful object, prone in the grass, and upon turning it over, he beheld a man with glassy eyes and sunken cheeks, a man so nearly starved to death that he could not speak or lift a hand. For two weeks he cared for this man. He nursed him step by step back to life and strength.

What happened next is not known; but it seems certain that the stranger, now recovered in health, slipped under cover of darkness to his sleeping benefactor and knocked his brains out with an axe. Then he mounted one of the miner's horses and rode away, and might well have escaped if some citizens of Salmon City had not soon discovered the murder and taken the trail. It was vigilantes who brought Bender into town, and they wanted to hang him immediately; but another, remembering a poster he had seen, recognized the man as Bender and pointed out that a huge reward had been offered for him. Some argued it was too much of a risk to try to take so desperate a fellow all the way to Kansas: and others said he ought to suffer for the crime committed here. A compromise was effected.

They took the man out and chained him to a stake in the backyard of a saloon. Here the miners gathered and tormented him with jeers and kicks, or strove to picture for him the fate that awaited him in Kansas. Bender was a coward, it seems: he worked himself into a prodigious panic and begged madly for his life. After the miners left him, he took his pocketknife, the only weapon he had, and slashed and hacked with it until he cut his chained foot off. How he endured the pain of cutting through the bone, of watching the blood spurt, without losing his senses, nobody could ever understand; but he did. And when free, he set

off, walking on his good foot and on the bloody stump, with
blood gushing around him. Blood showed that again and
again he pitched headlong, rose to his feet and struggled
on. But he did not go far. He bled to death and was found
the next morning in his own gore.

The citizens of Salmon now had a problem on their hands.
It was summertime; they could not ship the body and unless
they shipped it they could not receive the reward. An Indian
solved the problem. He said to bury the man in a swamp
until cold weather came. He was a witch doctor or something, and he said Bender would keep all right. And so they
buried him and marked the spot.

The remainder of the story still reads like the most incredible melodrama. The Indian double-crossed his white
friends. He robbed the marsh of the frightful corpse and
dragged it, dripping, out of the muck; and as he did so,
legend declares, one leg gave a spasmodic jerk. Thinking the
man still alive, the Indian buried his tomahawk in the skull
and then dragged the body off to the mountains to a secret
place. And there for hours he boiled it in a huge caldron,
watching intently the progress of his infernal stew. He was
making a medicine as an offering to his gods. After he
thought the body had boiled long enough, the Indian laid the
bones out to dry high in the limbs of a pine tree, and then
muttered his weird prayers.

Years passed, and the theft and the body were forgotten.
Then, one day, a miner found a skull in a tree and brought
it to town. Today, behind the bar in an old saloon, there is a
skull with the scar of an axe in one side of it. Is it Bender's
skull? Nobody knows.

Sheepherder Bill

Many stories are told about Sheepherder Bill, who, aside
from adding a touch of local color to the community on
various occasions, was in reality not much of an asset to
the town of Warren, although he gained quite a reputation
as a packer. Only five feet tall, he was of unusually powerful
build and on various occasions packed women and children
strapped to his back over Elk Summit. Among those who
were taken over the Summit by him in this manner were
Napier Edwards and Mrs. Abstein.

Bill liked his liquor and whenever he could sell a claim

or two he usually went to Boise on a bender. He didn't like
to drink alone so he'd hire a couple of men to drink with
him, but the minute they showed any signs of becoming intoxicated, they were fired. He landed in jail so often on
these sprees that, not liking the beds the city afforded, he
moved in one of his own. He had paid so many five-dollar
fines that one morning when he awakened to find himself
without the necessary funds, the judge took pity on him
and paid it for him. He had originally been educated to be
a preacher, and when the law picked him up it was usually
off a soapbox somewhere.

Down at the Rhodes ranch at New Meadows the boys
had caught a very young bear. The cub soon got on to all
sorts of tricks until finally someone had the bright idea of
teaching him how to box. He got so that every time anyone
came around he'd get up on his hind legs and start biffing
around. Once in awhile, when he got on one of his drunks,
Sheepherder Bill would wake up to find himself out in the
bed that had been built for the bear. Neither the bear nor
Bill seemed to mind the other's presence much.

One day a big Tennessean came to the ranch. He was
walking around the fields and happened to be standing by
an irrigation ditch when he looked around and saw a bear
coming at him. No one had warned him about the pet, and
when the bear started scuffling with him the fellow really
thought he meant business and started to fight for his life.
He managed to get the cub down in the irrigation ditch
and for more than an hour he worked in a vain endeavor to
get the bear's head under water long enough to drown him.
The bear finally squirmed away, got up, and trundled off toward home, but apparently he was not soon to forget the
incident.

The next time Sheepherder Bill came to the ranch on
his usual spree and went to sleep in the bear's box, he
awakened to find himself in the irrigation ditch with the
cub doing his best to drown him. He was so stupefied from
the effects of the liquor that only the efforts of the men who
had come over to see what the cub was up to saved him from
a watery grave.

But Bill was to come to a tragic end, anyway, and this
time there was to be no one there to save him. He had a
small log cabin up on the hill where he had been doing a
little moonshining on the side. Evidently, as nearly as any

one has ever been able to tell, the still blew up sometime during the night, setting the cabin on fire, and Bill burned with it.

An Act of God

In former times when Owyhee County was a thriving cattle country, two men were rounding up stray calves and branding them. One said: "If I've ever put a brand on a calf that wasn't mine, may lightning strike me dead!" Lightning struck him that afternoon. It killed his horse. On the man it left a blue mark on one temple. It ripped one boot open but did not injure the leg. Upon him was the odor of burnt flesh, but he did not die until several days later.

Yellow Dog Creek

Because members of the notorious Plummer gang used Chinese for target practice, a half-dozen Chinese men fled Virginia City and set out westward, seeking the Columbia River and the Coast. In crossing the mountains they were lost and wandered for weeks, feeding on roots and a few wild things that they killed with stones. After awhile they came upon two prospectors panning gold on a creek, slipped up on them, and murdered both, striking them down with clubs. Taking their provisions and gold, they resumed their journey, two of the Chinese putting on the shoes of the dead men. They had not gone far when they met several prospectors coming up the creek to join their companions; and upon observing the shoes of the murdered men, the prospectors forced the Chinese to return with them. Finding their dead companions, they shot the Chinese down one by one "for the yellow dogs that they were." Today the stream is known as Yellow Dog Creek.

"Him All Wight"[1]

Chinese believe that a person should die in his own home, if at all; and because of this superstition, a sick Chinese who, in the early days of Silver City, became very ill while visiting a friend was hustled out of the house. A doctor was called and declared that the man could not live through the night; whereupon the Chinese of the town held an excited

---

1 Told by an old Chinese of Silver City.

Yellow Dog Creek

conference and then took the sick man and wrapped him
in some old blankets and thrust him deep into a near-by
woodpile. The time was January. The next morning the
body was discovered, frozen as hard as a piece of ore. When
the sheriff questioned a Chinese, he said calmly, "Oh, him
go dead. Him fleeze to death. Him all wight."

A Lynching

There were thousands of Chinese in the vicinity of
Pierce in the early days. A storekeeper who had lived there
for many years and was very popular both at Lewiston and
at Pierce somehow had gained the bitter enmity of some of
the local Chinese organizations. It was not known what was
the cause of the trouble, but one morning when the storekeeper failed to appear, his friends investigated, to find he
had been butchered with hatchets. Apparently, he lived
alone at the rear of the store. There was blood all over the
walls. It was clearly a murder for revenge rather than
robbery, and there was little doubt in the minds of the
authorities but that it had been the work of some of the
local Chinese. To find the guilty parties was like looking
for a needle in a haystack. There was nothing to be learned
from the Chinese; none of them would talk.

Finally, someone remembered that up in Walla Walla
was an American who had been reared among the Chinese
and understood the language. His name was Lonny Sears.
The sheriff sent for Lonny, and in the meantime arrested ten
or fifteen of the most likely suspects and threw them all in
jail. When Sears arrived he was disguised as an Indian and
put in jail along with the Chinese on a pretended charge of
drunkenness. It soon became evident, as he listened to their
conversation, that the younger ones were endeavoring to put
the blame on some of the older ones. After a few days he had
all the evidence he required; six of the fifteen Chinese were
to be held and the others turned loose. For some reason, the
sheriff decided to move the six guilty Chinese from Pierce
to the jail at Lewiston.

The murdered storekeeper had many friends at Lewiston. The sheriff and his prisoners had gone only as far as
Weippe when they were met by a party of white men
disguised as Indians who succeeded in overpowering the
sheriff and taking his prisoners away from him. All six of

the Chinese were left dangling from the nearest tree. It was known that the men who did the hanging were friends of the murdered man and were from Lewiston, but nothing in the way of an investigation ever came of the matter.

Footnote to the Previous Story

In the early days of the wild mining town, Pierce City, when the population was seventeen thousand whites and three thousand Chinese, a white man was murdered, and seven Chinese, chained behind wagons, were led through the city. Then they were taken out a few miles and hanged one by one. Many years later, an old miner who had seen better days limped into town and confessed that he had murdered the man for whose slaying the seven had been lynched; and added that he had also been the leader of the mob that lynched them.

Death Names a Town

Plummer was named because of a most unusual circumstance. Many years ago, a small emigrant train camped on the site; and soon thereafter a black-bearded giant rode into the settlement on a stallion and dismounted and went to the door of a cabin. When a man answered the knock on the door, the stranger shot him dead, saying: "You dirty dog, you can't steal my wife!" A posse went in pursuit and overtook the man in the shadow of the Sun River Mountains in Montana. After a summary trial, the man was hanged. In a pocket was a letter addressed to "My Wife, Mrs. Jacqueline Plummer." News of the man hunt had gone abroad, and many letters poured into the village, addressed simply to Plummer, Idaho. In 1908 the town was named Plummer.

Curio Collector

Pinky Beard hated Indians, and when he entered town, the Indians stayed away. But Pinky never confessed during his life to the slaying of a redskin. He once said that he was on Cuddy Mountain and stopped by a creek to drink. "I noticed in the water the reflection of an Indian putting an arrow in his bow. It was a nice bow. Next time you're at my house I'll show it to you." He told of coming face to face with an Indian when rounding Council Mountain. And then his comment: "I believe that guy had one of the prettiest robes I ever saw." If you asked Pinky to tell more, he would only puff at his pipe and look at you. That he hated Indians as he hated rattlesnakes, and that he killed many of them, there seems no reason to doubt; but there is no proof. Pinky carried his secrets to his grave.

No William Tell

Kootenai County had an interesting political campaign in 1888. M. M. Musgrove told so many yarns about one of the Republican candidates that he was taken to task by Morris Green. In the encounter with fists Musgrove got all the worst of it and shot his opponent. The bullet knocked out a half-dozen of Green's teeth and loosened others; and with contempt for so clumsy a marksman he picked out the loosened teeth and hurled them in Musgrove's face. That was the end of the fight.

Skeleton Butte

Skeleton Butte in southern Idaho was formerly in the neighborhood of a wide-open mining town where Lew Landers played poker while his wife quietly sewed and waited in her cabin. Running into bad luck, he took a job on the building of the railroad, then coming across Idaho Territory, and one day received word that his wife had burned to death in her home. This blow almost destroyed Lew's sanity. He returned to gambling and drinking, but daily he could be seen reading the last letter he had received from her. When his money was gone, he heard that a liberal reward was offered for the return of a band of horses that had been stolen by notorious thieves who had their headquarters at the Devil's Corral. Alone, he set out to find the stolen beasts. He disappeared utterly, and nobody knew what had happened to him; but a year later the sheriff at Hailey received a letter declaring that on a butte the writer had found a skeleton. He investigated. The correspondent said he had been climbing the butte and had come first upon a boot with a man's foot in it, and then found bones and a skull. He found a coat and in a pocket of it the last letter Lew had ever received from his wife.

Missourians

A field worker asked an old-timer in Wallace what had put a stop to the labor troubles in that area. He told this story. Forty years ago several Missourians had come to the area to work in the mines. One afternoon, one of them, an old man, was basking on the station platform with his son. Three rowdies approached and heaped abuse upon all Missourians, whereupon the old man rose and hung his hat on a peg. His son murmured, "Mebbe I oughta—" and paused, lazily restoring his pipe to his mouth and relaxing his six feet three. The old man went into action and gave the rowdies the neatest licking they had ever taken. As the last man went down, the son removed his pipe and finished his sentence, "—told them they better not pick on pap."

Hardhat

Nineteen men and one woman reached the scene of a gold strike in the Coeur d'Alenes. A tent served as a saloon, the one log house being reserved for the woman. One evening she lifted the flap of the saloon tent and announced that she had shot Hardhat. There was no excitement. The men strolled over and observed that Hardhat was dead all right; he had been too drunkenly amorous, apparently, and had reached the end of his trail. A committee was appointed to serve in the capacity of a coroner. Its report of the circumstances did not mention Hardhat at all; but it did express regret that the cleaning up of the new camp had been left to a lady, and extended thanks to her for a job well done.

The Blue Bucket

More than half a century ago, a lone pioneer journeyed through Idaho on his way to Oregon and camped one night on Paradise Creek near Moscow. In filling his bucket with water from a creek, he scooped up gravel, and observed later that it was rich in gold. Being more interested in farming than in mining, he left the bucket and resumed his journey; but returned after a year, defeated in his agricultural efforts, to find the bucket and the rich placer deposits which he had left behind. He never found the Blue Bucket Mine, nor has anyone since, though many have searched for it.

Hardhat

The Last Look

During Silver City's turbulent existence, John Springer had a good deal of experience, serving as deputy sheriff under his brother Amos, and later under Charles M. Hayes and W. J. Hill. His duties consisted mainly in looking after the prisoners; and great was his amazement one day to learn that he had lost a horse thief. Springer at once took up the trail and headed for Sucker Creek and came presently to the ranch of Nat Graves. Explaining that he was on the trail of a thief, Springer asked Nat if he had seen anyone who looked suspicious.

"Well, yes," Graves said. A suspicious fellow had come to him and had asked where he could find a rowboat to cross Snake River. After directing him Graves thought he had better go count his own horses, and discovered that one was missing. So he took to the trail too. When he reached the river, the thief was in the boat and about halfway across. "When he saw me, why, he just raised up and plunged into the river headfirst." "He did?" said Springer. "That's what he done the last look I had at him." Springer saw a twinkle in Nat's eyes. He knew then that when Nat took his last look at the fleeing thief, he was gazing along the sights of his Winchester rifle.

A Love Story

Back in the sixties when Warren was the county seat of Idaho County, it was said to have had a population of from fifteen hundred to three thousand white people and from five hundred to three thousand Chinese. The Chinese eventually began to get such a hold on the mining industry that the white men took a hand in the matter and began a series of small persecutions that finally drove the majority of the Chinese out of the country, such as the time when three Chinese miners were strung up along the rafters of the old mill in Slaughter Gulch for the mere matter of having stolen a few pair of gum boots. Some of them, however, stayed on down through the years and played an important part in the later history of the camp.

Among the most interesting Chinese characters was a beautiful and very young Chinese slave girl who was later to become known as Polly Beamis. Polly was brought over

*A Love
Story*

from China in the slave traffic and was purchased in San Francisco by some of the Chinese who later landed at Warren.

Charlie Beamis, a gambler who was running a saloon in town at the time, had gotten into an argument with one of his customers over the settlement of a poker game. The man told Beamis if he didn't come to terms he'd shoot his eye out, which he very promptly proceeded to do. The bullet struck the bone at the corner of Charlie's eye, glanced, and plowed along the side of his head just above the ear. This bit of gunplay naturally put Beamis out of commission for some time, and during his illness it was Polly, the little slave girl, who nursed him back to health. Polly was gradually getting out from under the domination of her former master, and the two fell madly in love with each other. Some months later, Beamis married Polly, and they were said to have been the happiest couple in town.

Finally, they moved to a ranch on the South Fork of the Salmon and lived there for thirty years before Beamis died. There had been a great love between the two, and Polly became broken-hearted and lost, spending her time between Warren and Grangeville and the old home. On her last visit to Boise before her death she visited some of the Chinese families, but she had almost completely forgotten her own language. In her last illness she asked to be taken home to be buried beside her husband, and was said to have been buried in Grangeville in 1923.

The Devil Himself

Some old-timers contend that the Indians do not hold to belief in a personal devil, as do Christians, but others refute this by stories such as the following:

In 1902 Charlie Ross lived in the area around Inkom. He was a huge man with a terrifying black beard and the appearance of an honest-to-goodness villain. The Indians in this region had a village and one day conducted a very solemn ceremony within their stockade. Curious, Charlie and a friend went to the board fence and peered through; whereupon almost at once there was a pandemonium inside. and the Indians fled. That night they completely moved their village to a new location, explaining that during their ceremony the devil himself had looked in upon them.

Stampede Lake

Not far from Naples is Stampede Lake, which, according to legend, got its name from the following circumstance. A freighting outfit was attacked by a band of Kootenai Indians who abducted one of the men as well as the livestock. The freighters started in pursuit and came to the charred corpse of a man, tied to a tree; around the "horror pine" smoking embers told the story. On the bank of the lake the freighters overtook the Indians and literally stampeded them into the lake, shooting or drowning every one of them.

Light Sun and Leading Star

The chief of the Shoshoni Indians, who lived on the bank of the Snake River, was a very old man and was very kind to his people. He had a young son named Light Sun who liked to hunt in the forest. One time Light Sun went into the forest to hunt, and he met a young Indian girl who was very pretty. They hunted together in the forest for animals for a long time; then they went to her people and told them she wanted to marry the young warrior. Her people consented, and they went to his tribe and were married.

The old chief liked the young maiden very much and when he died he gave to her instead of to his son the royal blanket. She ruled with her husband's help and she was known as Leading Star. They had four children, two girls and two boys, who grew up to be fine and sturdy men and women.

Leading Star died when she was sixty-nine years old, and her husband Light Sun ruled. He was as kind to the people as his father and wife had been.

He died soon after the first wagon train came to his tribe. His last word was haw—meaning hello, the only English word he knew.

Three-Fingered Smith

Three-Fingered Smith was one of the earliest settlers on the South Fork of the Salmon. He came by his title from the fact that when bitten on the hand by a rattlesnake, he seized an axe and chopped off the two fingers that had been struck. This was only one of his many misfortunes. His

Three-Fingered Smith

fifteen-year-old son, who carried the mail to the Cleveland mine, sat down one day to rest and froze to death. His wife ran away with a sailor and left a family of several children for the father to take care of.

One day a band of marauding Indians came along and ran off with a bunch of Smith's horses. He and his neighbors pursued and overtook them near Cascade; but as the whites were making camp, the Indians attacked and killed three of the men. Smith, badly wounded, crawled on his hands and knees for thirty-five miles to the cabin of old "Juice-Harp" Jack.

Smith recovered and then went to Florence, where he struck a rich mine; and thereupon moved to Warren, where he is said to have spent one hundred thousand dollars in one hundred days. He'd buy an entire saloon for a night and turn it over to his friends; and if they didn't like the brands of liquor there, he'd buy another saloon. The money which he found it impossible to spend for saloons he gave away. He is said to have made a second fortune on Slaughter Gulch and to have spent it as he spent the first. He died a pauper.

One of his sons lives on the old place on the South Fork.

A Famous Judge

Warren has long been a wild town. As late as 1918 two women got into a scrape there and before they were done with it, the whole town was involved. Andy Kavanaugh, who lived there for forty years and was judge and justice of the peace for twenty-six years, achieved fame when Ripley put him in his "Believe-It-Or-Not" as the only judge in the United States who had never assessed a fine. As a matter of fact, Ripley erred: Kavanaugh did assess one; it was on his own bondsman, Brad Carey, for illegal transportation of deer meat.

Of the many interesting cases that came before the judge, the following is typical. A woman swore out a complaint of nonsupport against her husband, who was known among his fellow sufferers by the name of Van. Van had a friend and sympathizer who owned a saloon and went by the name of Doug. Things looked pretty tough for Van when Doug went before the judge and swore by the stars and moon that it would be a crime to throw Van into jail. Deciding that there was nothing like whisky to put a judge into a humor, Doug fetched several bottles to court; and though the judge saw through his strategy, he drank freely nevertheless. "Down with liquor!" he roared, and down it went. After a while he became so happy that he decided to adjourn court and move over to Doug's saloon, but he was still an old fox. At the moment when Doug and Van thought things had turned their way, the judge remembered the case before him and arrived at a decision. As drunk as a lord but as solemn as an owl, he declared that Van must serve ninety days in jail and pay a fine of two hundred dollars—if he ever married another woman!

Van never married again.

Postscripts to a Bad End

In the days of the notorious Plummer, a bad hombre named Clark shot a boy in cold blood and was acquitted. Feeling ran high; and, fearing the man would be lynched, the sheriff rushed him to Boise and put him into the guardhouse there, but a few days later he was found hanging dead from makeshift gallows beyond the present Memorial Bridge south of the business section of the city.

That was the end of Clark for a long while. Many years later, a steamship company in Portland auctioned off unclaimed baggage and among the items was a large case that caused much interest. The bidding on it was spirited; and after a man named Mitchell acquired it, a crowd gathered, eager to learn what he had bought. When the case was broken open, they saw to their amazement the mummified corpse of a man. Mitchell didn't know what to do with him: he had bought the dead fellow and according to the law had to pay for the burial. He was particularly chagrined to learn that he had bought all that was left of Clark, the infamous bad man.

Not His Brother's Keeper[1]

Sixty years ago, two brothers in a famous Idaho mining area had a pert thirteen-year-old sister who was in school. She was known as a mischief maker. In any case, she reported one day that her teacher had made insulting remarks to her. The girl's father called on him, and the teacher vehemently denied the charge and said he would be willing to go before the trustees. There the matter rested for some time.

But one day the two brothers were seen coming into town, one riding and the other walking, and when the teacher in the hotel barroom was warned, he seized a rifle and went to the porch to meet them. The brother who was walking hid behind the mule and leveled his gun and shot the teacher squarely between the eyes; whereupon with no hesitation at all, he turned and shot his own brother in the stomach. It was argued later that he intended to make out that the teacher had shot his brother, and so justify his murder of the teacher.

The brother shot in the stomach did not die at once. The other came to him one night and said, "It's just too blamed bad that worthless teacher shot you." The sick man shook his head and answered: "No, he didn't shoot me. It was you." The wounded brother died; and the other, after standing trial, was acquitted. Thereupon he fled to Texas and the remainder of this story is legendary. It is said that he was obsessed by the notion that two men were on his

---

1 Names and places are not given, out of deference to surviving relatives.

Not His Brother's
Keeper

trail; and one day, unable any longer to endure his fear and agony of soul, he looked in a mirror and shot himself between the eyes.

Some Schoolteachers Were Tough

Johnny Hughes was a schoolteacher, and a peaceful chap when sober; but when he was filled with whisky he did strange things. From a mild-mannered gentleman he leapt into the role of an honest-to-goodness bad man and wanted to raise Cain with all the guns he could find. One of his best friends was Mike Nellis, more commonly known as McNellis; but Johnny paid no attention to friendship when he got soaked to the gills.

One day, with fire in his belly and blood in his eye, he made for the Magnolia Saloon, but stopped at the hotel to ask the landlady a question: "If I furnish a corpse will you go to the funeral?" The woman thought he was trying to be funny and told him to go on about his business, but Johnny was not trying to be funny at all. He was out to get Mike Nellis and he meant business. Mike meant business, too, when he saw Johnny coming, and he lost no time in getting into action. He made a dive for Johnny; and as he clutched with one hand the arm holding the gun, he drew a knife with his other and buried it thirteen times to the hilt in Johnny before he decided he had done enough. Johnny was dead when he hit the floor. Friendship made way for a gun or a knife in them-there days!

An Early Sheriff

Back in the days when for a brief while Idaho City was the Territory's metropolis, the penitentiary was there, full of gamblers and gunmen of all sorts. A man named Gorman, first a deputy and later sheriff, was a fearless fellow, but he relied chiefly on a persuasive tongue.

One day there was a break at the prison, and several men escaped. After all but one or two had been captured, Gorman mounted his horse and set off alone. He had a pretty good idea of the direction one of the men had taken, and because the snow was deep he believed he could track him easily. As he rode along he whistled and made as much noise as he could, not wanting to surprise the fellow into an attack; and when he found the fleeing man, he was ready, as Gorman had surmised he would be, with his guns primed and cocked.

Gorman told him not to get excited, for he had no intention of taking him back. He merely wanted to see if he was all right and in good health and to pass the time of day with him. That, he added, was all he was paid to do as an officer and a gentleman. And so in his easy humorous way he talked and talked until the escaped convict relaxed his vigilance and began to grin. Anyway, Gorman didn't seem to have a gun on him, so why should he stand there with a pistol in either hand? When Gorman said he guessed he'd dismount and tighten his cinch a bit before starting home, the beguiled fellow offered no protest. Gorman dismounted, threw a stirrup over the saddle, and in the next instant had jerked a gun from a saddlebag and had the muzzle pointing steadily at the man he was after. Dropping his guns with a yell of rage and raising his hands, the flabbergasted man shouted:

"Oh, you, why didn't I kill you when I had you!"

March of Empire

Former U. S. Senator Dubois was a diplomat; and in consequence of his tact and his sense of humor, he was sometimes sent out from Washington to iron out troubles with the Indians at Fort Hall. One mission was particularly difficult: Uncle Sam wanted more land, and the Senator's job was to make the Indians like their Uncle's greediness.

After Dubois had gathered about him all the chief Indians of the council, the pipe of peace was passed, with the dark-skinned warriors solemnly puffing and waiting, each face as expressionless as granite. Then through an interpreter the Senator spoke, declaring that the Great White Father desired some more of their land. After he was done he waited expectantly for an answer, but there was only complete and oppressive silence. Then, to his amazement, one of the Indians began to speak in excellent English.

"You say the Great White Father who resides in Washington wants some more of our land?" The Senator assured him that his ears had not deceived him. The Great White

Father had urgent need of more land and wanted some right here. "Well," said the Indian, "what in hell's the use of talking about it? He'll take it anyway."

When Did Buffalo Horn Die?[1]

Many stories have been told of the death of Buffalo Horn, and it has been generally assumed that he was killed at the battle of South Mountain. His "bones" were found, and at least a half-dozen men have declared that they shot him. There is no doubt that he was shot, but there is no trustworthy proof that he died on the battlefield. None of his warriors, some of whom are still living, saw him die, and none of them positively declare that he was killed in that memorable battle.

In Arnold's version of the story (Indian Wars of Idaho), Buffalo Horn was an intelligent and ambitious leader who had been given command of a group of Bannack scouts under the leadership of General Howard, and had been instrumental in effecting Chief Joseph's surrender. Later, he became angry with Howard and left him to go to Fort Hall, where he tried to incite the Bannacks to rebellion. He went also to other reservations, and after recruiting Indians there, he returned to Fort Hall in May of 1878. Accompanied by several warriors, he set forth to join Chief Egan and his Piutes on the Malheur Reservation at Stein's Mountain in Oregon. Near Glenns Ferry he killed several white men, stole cattle, and headed for Silver City. Meanwhile, word had reached Silver City of the massacre, and of the murder of Fletcher Hawes at Big Springs. A company of volunteers under Captain Harper set forth to meet the Indians. Among the Indian scouts in this expedition was Piute Joe.

The volunteers arrived in the neighborhood of South Mountain, where they were attacked by Horn and his warriors. Harper tried to stand them off; but upon seeing that he was outnumbered three to one he gave orders to retreat, and was fleeing with his men when a bullet knocked Buffalo Horn from his horse. Thereupon the Indians stopped to take care of their fallen leader, and the volunteers escaped. Piute Joe maintained that he was the man who toppled the chieftain. Arnold says: "Joe's story was never verified, for in the excitement of such thrilling moments men's nerves are

---

[1] This account is based on the research of Violet Eggers.

strung to the highest tension, and to tell who fired that fatal shot would be a matter of conjecture."

In Pocatello is a Mrs. Blakeslee, one of Buffalo Horn's cousins; she is the daughter of a Texas ranger who married a squaw. She says Buffalo Horn did not die at South Mountain, but escaped and went to Wyoming. She was only a child at the time, but she remembers a stranger who came to her mother's, and that her mother called him only by the name of brother. According to her, Horn's identity was closely guarded and only after he left two years later did her father tell her who the man was. It is true that the Indians had a period of prolonged mourning for their dead chief, but Mrs. Blakeslee says this was to outwit federal officials who were hot on Horn's trail.

Mrs. Blakeslee declares further that Buffalo Horn had a bullet in his spine and suffered much agony before recovering from his wound. After awhile he became homesick and returned to Fort Hall; but his appearance had changed a great deal. The bullet had caused him to stoop, and he was not recognized. At Fort Hall he pretended to be a Shoshoni and became known as Piccua (meaning stooped over), and lived there until his death in 1915.

The only evidence that Buffalo Horn died at South Mountain was a skeleton which was declared to have been his. Old-timers in Silver City, if asked how they know Horn died there, say that a skeleton was found near the spot where he was supposed to have been shot. Residing at Fort Hall is Billy George, an Indian scout who accompanied Buffalo Horn: he says Horn was not fatally wounded, and that the skeleton was another man. He points out that the Indians would never have abandoned a wounded chief, and especially when the enemy was in full flight. George says that Horn, with twenty picked scouts, was riding along a ridge when they saw the volunteers from Silver City, who at once began firing. Horn and his warriors rode swiftly toward them, whereupon the whites dismounted, fired one volley, remounted, and fled. At this moment Horn observed that one of the Indian scouts with the white party had been left behind, and he began circling around the Indian who, taking steady aim, fired at Horn and knocked him off his horse. George says Horn was wounded in his leg but admits that the bullet could have taken an upward course to the man's spine because of the crouching position in which he was riding. He adds that Horn was taken back to camp where he asked to be left, urging his warriors to go at once to join Egan's forces. George says they left him in camp, and whether he died there he does not know. If he died there, his grave has never been found.

When some of the older residents on the Fort Hall reservation were interviewed, they admitted that an Indian had lived there under the name of Piccua. Records of deaths twenty-three years ago were poorly kept, and in consequence it has not been possible to learn where or when Piccua was buried. Some say he was buried in the graveyard known as the Hill of Humans two miles west of Fort Hall, but many tombstones here are unmarked and unidentified.

Old-timers of Silver City give no credit to Piute Joe. Some say it was Oliver Purdy who fired the shot, and some say it was Nick Maher. Nick Maher told Lish Lewis that he was the man, but he did not say that he killed the chief. Sally Winnemucca, in her story of life among the Piutes, tells of having met Piute Joe shortly after the battle and of his assuring her that he shot Buffalo Horn. It is not at all strange that several men have laid claim to the distinction of having shot a notorious renegade Indian chief, whose grave is unknown.

A resident of Salmon City tells a story to prove that you can't identify a man by a pile of bones. In the early days, Si Ferrin and a bunch of riders were gathering cattle when they came upon the bones of a man. They dismounted and buried the bones and notified the coroner, who told them that they had acted properly, and paid them for the burial. Later, they came upon other skeletons and buried them and were rewarded handsomely; whereupon it occurred to them that they had hit upon a most lucrative racket. Soon, however, they ran out of bones; and when, wishing to celebrate, but finding themselves out of funds, they dug up a skeleton, they discovered that they would have to complete it with bones from animals. As soon as they had done so, they sent for the coroner, but the gullible fellow had begun to come to his senses. He gazed down at the skeleton and shook his head sadly. "I'm afraid, boys," he said, "we'll have to call this a jackass."

The skeleton found on South Mountain was not that of a jackass, and almost as certainly it was not that of Buffalo Horn.

A Man of His Word

Mike Rock, the fighting Irish sheriff of Owyhee County, was one of the best-known officers of early times. Persons learned that he meant business and that he always gave fair warning. "By hell," he'd say, "mind what I'm tellun yez. Ye better watch out!"

A short and powerful man, he depended more on his fists than on a gun. During the trouble at the Coeur d'Alene mines a bunch of rough fellows blew into Silver City; and on Labor Day they got drunk and caused a riot. Mike closed his big tough hands and waded in. After knocking out four of the men and dragging them by their heels to the jail, he was bashed on the head with a bottle by the fifth man. A little dazed, Mike chased him down the street and knocked him over and threw him into a cell with his companions. "Mind what I'm tellun yez," said he. "Ye can't get away with it!"

Generous, he was often imposed on by unscrupulous friends. Once he lent money to a man named Greene; and upon learning that Greene had hit the grit without paying, Mike mounted his old horse, Baldy, and followed the stage to Nampa. When Greene got off he received the flogging of his life. "By hell," said Mike, returning to Silver City, "they can't get away with it, I'm tellun yez!"

Woodruff the Outlaw[1]

Fred Woodruff, a teamster, was a quiet person when sober, but when drunk he had a face as ugly as woe. With murder in his eye he would boast that he'd play any game from seven-up to manslaughter. Tiring of being a teamster, he entered partnership with Lige Calk and Chipp Reager and embarked on a lusty career of horse stealing, with headquarters in a deep canyon on the North Folk of the Owyhee River. He hired a young man named Wilson to look after his stolen horses, and everything went along in good horse-thief style until one day when Wilson recognized among a new herd some beasts that belonged to a former benefactor, Bill Maher. As soon as Woodruff was out of sight, Wilson turned the horses loose, knowing that they would go back to their home range.

---

1 Based on the story of Lish Lewis, Silver City, one of the men who tried to stop the fire.

When Woodrug learned what happened he was as angry and ugly as he could be. The best thing to do, he decided, was to sock Wilson away; and at once he called Calk and Reager and drew lots to learn who would do the killing. The job fell to Reager.

Several days later, Wilson was cooking a meal when Reager was alone with him. Woodruff appeared on the scene and took Reager aside and asked why in thunder he had not bumped the fellow off. Thus rebuked, Reager yanked his gun out and fired, but at that moment Wilson turned and the bullet only grazed his cheek. Out of patience, Woodruff seized the pistol and shot the young man down in cold blood. With Wilson out of the way, Woodruff continued his raids more daringly than before, and was smart enough to keep several jumps ahead of the ranchers.

Again matters drifted prosperously until some of Wilson's friends set out to look for him. John Springer, sheriff at the time, joined the search. Calk turned State's evidence when Woodruff was arrested. After Woodruff was lodged in jail he discovered that his only companion was a Chinese who had stolen an armful of shingles. No guard was placed over the two men, because the snow was deep and if they had escaped they could not have gone far.

On Easter Sunday, April 13, 1884, two men living on the second floor of the jail heard a terrific din below. The Chinese thief was yelling for all he was worth. The men ran down to report to the sheriff, and he and several others started for the jail in a blinding snowstorm. It was not until they reached the door that they discovered the jail to be a raging furnace. Sam Slick dashed in and rescued the man named James Lyman, who was already overcome by smoke; but Woodruff and the Chinese were beyond rescue. Woodruff had locked the Chinese in his cell and then fired the jail; whereupon he retired to his own cell and cut his throat.

It is known that Woodruff had a sardonic sense of humor; and it is supposed that, knowing he would be hanged, he decided to do the job himself. He locked the poor yelping Chinese fellow in and burned him up, doubtless because it seemed to him a humorous thing to do.

The jail was in the courthouse. The story of the burning of this building has never before been published.

A Bad Father-in-Law

When Pocatello was only a store and a saloon, Perry Pleasant was well liked by everybody around town. He married a girl from Marsh Valley. Her father was a constable.

Little was known of Perry's history before he came to Idaho from Texas; but he was so generally liked that it came as a shock and surprise to his friends to learn that he was wanted in Texas for murder. He had been in some sort of jam, and in making his escape from the posse had shot and killed two of the men who were after him. A reward of five thousand dollars was being offered by the state of Texas for his capture.

Perry's wife, in a moment of anger at her husband, had told the truth to her father. Whether it was the lure of the reward or his sense of duty that impelled him is not known; but Perry returned home one night to find his father-in-law a self-appointed one-man reception committee with a shotgun. The old man had the drop on Perry and there didn't seem to be much that he could do about it. Finally, he asked the old man if he could roll a cigarette. Receiving his permission, Perry rolled it, and stooping over to strike a match on his boot, swift as lightning from out of his boot he drew his six-shooter. Both men fired at the same instant. Both men fell dead.

The Malad Divide Robbery

About 1870 a rather daring hold-up was staged in the vicinity of Malad Divide, approximately ten miles north of the town of Malad. A man of many aliases, one of which was Ed Flag, and a gent by the name of Stone succeeded in holding up the Wells, Fargo stage and getting away with two bars of gold valued at forty-five thousand dollars. They had rigged up a couple of dummies or scarecrows and so placed them by the side of the road as to give the stage driver the impression that there were four men instead of two. While the hold-up was being staged they kept up a continual conversation. Accordingly, the stage driver, in reporting the robbery, informed the authorities that there were four men in the party.

A seven-man posse took up the trail on Friday night.

The men must have felt pretty secure, because they had made no effort to cover their trail. Part of the posse had gone down in the direction of Cache Valley and the others, still on the lookout for four men, had come across the trail left by the robbers, which showed the tracks of three horses and two men. Finally, they came to the place where the robbers had camped and found evidence that led them to believe they were on the right track. Nearing the place where they thought the robbers must be in hiding, three of the men were left to guard the horses. Just as Oakley shouted a warning to Robbins, a shot rang out, and Robbins fell to the ground dead. Oakley killed the man who was known as Flag, and shot the other robber in the leg.

Stone confessed and disclosed the hiding place of the gold. He was sent to the penitentiary at Boise, but served only a short time before he was pardoned. He thereupon became a preacher.

Doc Rooker Doings

In the good old days when Pocatello was a wide-open Western place, its best-known character was Doc Rooker, county coroner and popular man about town.

Up at Lava, an Italian had killed a section boss by the name of Pat McNamara. He had been arrested and was languishing in jail awaiting trial. Doc and a friend decided to play a game of cards, with the corpse of the prisoner at stake. He was going to hang anyway, and apparently there was some argument as to the disposal of the remains. If Doc lost, he was to put up one hundred dollars to see that the man was given a burial, befitting if not a scholar and a gentleman, at least a man of unerring aim. If Doc won, he was to get the corpse of the doomed man to do with as he damned well pleased. As it turned out, Doc found himself with a corpse on his hands.

But the doomed man was not to hang! Along about four o'clock one morning the spirit of the apparently healthy doomed one took its departure from its earthly shell in a most mysterious manner. It might have been that Phelps, a man of action, resented the idea of languishing with nothing more interesting than the hangman's noose to look forward to.

The body was evidently then dedicated to science and

the noble efforts of a couple of medical students. After they had finished with it, Doc stepped up and claimed the skeleton. Being a man somewhat mischievous by nature, he and his skeleton together put the fear of the Lord into the hearts of many a man with a hangover. He would hide the skeleton or some part of it under his overcoat and take a walk down to the saloon—to show it suddenly to the horrified gaze of the bystanders. The barkeeper himself began to develop a bad case of jitters and a sudden desire to depart in haste for parts unknown.

On one occasion, a Negro swamper who had been looking after Doc's office all unsuspecting opened a closet door only to have the skeleton topple out and on him. He, too, took to the brush in a hurry, and in those days the brush was still growing close to Center Street.

Doc usually browsed forth in a top hat and a swallow-tailed coat, a handsome figure of a man, about six feet two. He was something of a gun-toter and a crack shot himself.

On one occasion he and a couple of his friends were careening somewhat crookedly down the street when Doc found himself suddenly confronted by the figure of a wooden Indian so much used as a sign by cigar stores in the early days. The stoic and dignified solemnity of the Indian's expressionless countenance must have been too much for Doc in his hilarious mood. In any case, he pulled out his gun and took a shot at the statue. It must have had a disastrous effect, for the shooter was called upon the mat, and Doc declared it to have been purely a matter of self-defense, and his loyal friends swore that such was the case.

Murder in Murphy

Murphy, now the seat of Owyhee County, and still as near the frontier as any other village in the State, hasn't much to boast of in hell-roaring episodes. Old-timers there do remember when Nick Kaurish, justice of the peace, could not find a Bible, and so married a couple with a Montgomery Ward catalog. They remember also that he got mixed up in his names and married the best man instead of the bridegroom.

The nearest thing to a shooting scrape was Jake Fletcher's dastardly murder of Jim Weiss. The two men were in Nick's Saloon when they fell to scuffling and trying

to shove one another outside; and Dave Pritchard, lying
by the stove trying to sleep off a bender, rose in alarm and
watched them. On hands and knees he implored the men to
shake hands and forget their quarrel, but they only brawled
the more lustily. Going to the rear of the building, Dave
told the constable that two men were trying to slay one
another, and the constable forthwith deputized Dave, told
him to stop the fight, and went back to sleep. Dave returned
and persuaded the two warriors to go home.

The next morning he was horrified to learn that Jake had
shot Jim. Jim was dying in the rear of the saloon and sent
word that he wanted to say good-by to Dave. When Dave
entered the darkened room and saw the blood-soaked bed,
he fell to his knees and began to pray. After praying with
all his might, he gave five dollars to help buy flowers, said
good-by to the dying man, and went around the town,
wringing his hands and telling everyone that Jake had
killed Jim. It was ten days later when he learned that the
whole thing had been a hoax, and that the realistic touch
had been gained by some blood from the butchershop.

Judges Are Like That

Murphy still talks of the case of Jake Rubin versus
Charlie Drawn. Jake had a fine big ranch on Sinker Creek
when along came Charlie to jump a part of the claim and
to steal a part of the water for irrigation. Rubin hardly
knew what to do about that; but after Charlie reached out
for more land, Jake decided he would have to sue the man
or shoot him. He decided to sue him.

The case came up before Raleigh Latham, justice of the
peace, who found Charlie guilty and fined him ten dollars.
When the justice learned that Charlie didn't have ten dollars, he pondered the matter and fined Jake ten dollars, de-
termined to get the money from someone to pay court costs.
Court costs were chiefly the drinks. When the astounded
Jake dug up ten dollars, the justice went over to the saloon
and bought drinks for the house. Jake was feeling pretty
sore about the whole thing. It was too much to be fined for
winning his own case. But according to those who remember
the case, he did nothing save to walk up to the judge and say,
"Latham, you got one damn bum court!"

A Big Jim Episode

Big Jim, a renegade Indian, terrorized the women and children around Silver City for many years by entering their homes when the men were away and commanding the women to cook meals for him. When not bumming meals, he was usually drunk; and one day, full of whisky, he set out for Oreana and froze to death. When the Indians learned of it there was great wailing. Ed Keevney and Tom Winchester told the Indians on Castle Creek and at once they set out to get the corpse. Ed had ridden a bronco that had worn himself out with bucking. It was decided to let Big Jim's squaw ride the horse and she mounted, with one child behind her and a papoose in a crib tied to the saddlehorn.

Everything was all right until something frightened the bronco. Unaccustomed to flying shawls and flapping skirts, the beast rolled his eyes and decided to unload. And unload he did, with the poor squaw sailing in one direction, the child in another, and both fetching up with a terrific yell. More scared than ever, the horse bucked himself out of sight and the squaw shouted that she had a papoose tied to the saddle horn. When the horse was caught, however, no papoose was on it; nor were the men able to find the child for two hours. Then they were amazed. There, flat on its back under a sagebrush, was the papoose, sucking its thumb and gurgling as if the whole affair had been great fun.

Clark's Folly

F. L. Clark has become one of the principal legends of northern Idaho. Fable, in an attempt to explain him, says he owned a gold mine reaching from Brazil to Alaska. In any case, this strange and wealthy man arrived one day in northern Idaho and tried to buy Hayden Lake; and failing in that, he bought several hundred acres along the south shore and built an enormous mansion. He built and launched on the lake a boat that could have sailed the seven seas; planted rare flowers, one of which is said to have cost him two thousand dollars; and lived among his eighty-five rooms. The walls were covered with hand-painted paper imported from France at five hundred dollars a roll; the glazed tile inlay in the brick walls was from Italy, and is said to have cost a fabulous price. The road across his estate was walled with hand-faced stone.

Twenty-two house servants and ninety-eight outside workers were employed. Nevertheless, all this extravagance failed to please the lady of his choice, and suddenly he vanished, and for eight years nothing was known of his whereabouts. Then he was discovered living in an isolated hermitage on an island in the Pacific Ocean. He was persuaded to return to Idaho and resume management of his estate, but his sojourn was short, and again he disappeared. Rumors of him have come back, the most persistent of which declares he is the head of a large mining company in Brazil. His great house is now barricaded with many gates and hung with No Trespassing signs. The owner is still an enigma. Some find an answer to his strange personality in the fact that the once bright green shutters are decorated with tiny hearts.

The Saga of Peg-Leg Annie

This woman also has passed into legend, though the circumstances of her life are well known. She was only four when her father, Steve McIntyre, carried her on his back into the mining camp of Rocky Bar, July 4, 1864. Her father, one of the owners of the Golden Star mine, a huge gold producer, was later killed in a street brawl. Annie became a tall lovely girl with dark hair and thoughtful brown eyes, and, later, the owner of a restaurant and rooming house. It is still said of her that she had one of the biggest hearts in Idaho and never turned a hungry person from her door. It is said, too, that she could take care of herself, and often yanked her pistol and fired a few shots into the ceiling when her patrons became tough, and swore as picturesquely as any. She was the Calamity Jane of the area.

It was perhaps in the year 1898 when she and Mrs. Emma Von Losch started afoot across Bald Mountain from Atlanta to Rocky Bar. Emma was a Bavarian, on her way home to visit her people. On the day they left, Bill Tate, a mail carrier, left on his regular route to Bald Mountain cabin on Atlanta summit. He passed Annie and Emma, five miles out; and when he exchanged mail with Bob Jackson on the summit, he said the two women were on their way south. The women did not arrive. Three days passed before a searching party could be sent out; and halfway

The Saga of
Peg-Leg Annie

down Bald Mountain on the northern slope a crew came upon an amazing sight. Crawling around on frozen hands and knees was Annie, half-crazed from hunger and cold and muttering to herself. She sounded like an animal out of the jungles.

She was taken to Atlanta and a doctor was summoned from Mountain Home; but Mountain Home was eighty miles south and something had to be done at once. So Annie was filled with whisky and tied down, and a man named Tug Wilson took a jackknife and common meat saw and cut her frozen legs off above the ankles. Annie lay without a murmur and watched him. When her mind cleared, she told of what had happened. She and Dutch Emma had fortified themselves with whisky as long as it lasted, and then, in the second night, Emma had frozen to death. Annie had taken her underwear off to cover the dead woman. Then, half out of her mind, she set off for help. When a rescue party went to get Emma, they found her as stiff as a log; and once the hard body got away from them and rolled clear to the bottom of the mountain before it was recovered.

Annie got well, and for awhile hobbled around her restaurant on her stumps. She still managed her business and she still fired the pistol when necessary. Later, she earned enough money to buy artificial legs, but as likely as not she would lay them aside and walk on her stumps, finding her wooden legs, she said, more of a nuisance than a help. She had five children when she made the journey to Bald Mountain. They grew up and scattered, and for twenty-two years she lived with an Italian who went under the name of Henry Longheme. He had a saloon next to her restaurant. During these years she saved nearly $12,000. In 1924, when Longheme set out to visit his folks in Italy, she entrusted the money to him to be deposited in a San Francisco bank. She never heard from him again, she never saw her money, but she persisted to the end in believing that he had been robbed and killed. During her last years she was supported by friends.

Many are the legends that have grown up around her name. One of them declares that she was furious when she learned that Wilson had sawed her legs off carelessly, so that one was longer than the other. Annie could curse like a pirate and shoot like a man; but she had a heart of gold and still shines like the sun in the memory of those who knew her.

Diamond Field Jack

The trial of Diamond Field Jack is one of the epic cases of its kind in the history of the State, and marked the last great fight between sheepmen and cattlemen. Jack Davis was a colorful character in the Nevada gold-rush days. A noted gunman, he was also a noted teller of tall tales; and it was chiefly his boasting of himself as a desperate fellow that led to his arrest for the murder of two sheepmen.

At the trial, W. E. Borah and the District Attorney argued for the State, and J. H. Hawley for the defense. There were no witnesses and very little evidence against the accused man; but sheepmen declared that Diamond Field Jack had visited their camps and made threats to kill the whole outfit if the sheepmen didn't clear out of the cattle country.

The trial became a notorious one; feeling ran high. Jack had once worked for the Sparks-Herrel outfit in Nevada; and Sparks, governor of the State, came to the defense of his former employee. Nevertheless, Jack was convicted on circumstantial evidence and sentenced to hang at Albion, though at the last minute Hawley obtained a reprieve.

Of this reprieve, three copies were made, and sent to Albion by three armed messengers, each taking a different route. Jack remained in jail for awhile, but was finally pardoned, whereupon he returned to Nevada and became wealthy. Some old-timers say Governor Sparks of Nevada made two unsuccessful attempts to bribe the court, offering a hundred thousand dollars for the release of the prisoner.

The Fortune of Luke Billy[1]

Another tale that sounds reasonable is of the money that the old Nez Perce Indian, Luke Billy, left near his old home on Billy Creek. Where the Boise Trail crosses Salmon River at the mouth of Billy Creek was the home of Luke Billy. His father had lived there for years, and here Luke Billy was born and grew to manhood. It is a pleasant little valley with a lot of good water and plenty of firewood. The winters were pleasant and the grass grew tall, an ideal home for the Indians, and Luke Billy grew very wealthy in horses and cattle. His herds roamed over the Salmon River coun-

---

1 By John L. Rooke, Cottonwood.

try and spread to the Camas Prairie, and his brand LB was
well known to all stockmen in the country. When the
soldiers came to Fort Lapwai, he sold many cattle to the
soldiers, always receiving his pay in gold coins. He was a
fine-looking big Indian with his two long braids of hair
dangling down in front. He was honored by both the whites
and Indians. I knew him as late as 1924, and at that time
he was in his eighties, but as straight as an arrow. He had
become a Catholic, and made his home in later years near
the Slickapoo Mission in the Lapwai Valley. For years
before he died, he would make trips back to Billy Creek
every summer, and he would always return with enough
twenty-dollar gold pieces to last until the next summer. The
Indians believe that he had cached his wealth somewhere
near Billy Creek. Indians have told me that some of them
tried to track him to see where he went, but this wise old
gentleman was too smart for the younger generation of
Nez Perces and they always lost him. He traveled light.
I remember meeting him on the mountain above Billy Creek
when he was riding a big bay horse, and he did not seem to
have any baggage except a pair of saddlebags on the back
of his saddle. It is a well-known fact that he sold a lot of
cattle and received many twenty-dollar gold pieces. It must
have run into many thousands of dollars, but when he died
there was very little money. So the question is, did he bury
his money on Billy Creek? If he did, we believe that it still
waits for the lucky man. Luke Billy (or Billy Luke, as some
called him) was a gentleman and a warrior and if he hid
his money, he hid it well.

Pioneer Humor[1]

It seems that there was a certain brand of humor among
the early settlers and pioneers, as they were seldom too busy
or tired to take time off and work hard to play some prank
on their friends. That is one of the things which seem to
be missing among the present generation. I suppose that
they are too busy making money and that it is such a serious
business that there is no time for such foolishness in the
present scheme of things. As I recall the wit and humor
that was in the make-up of the early settlers of this country
I cannot help thinking that the present generation is missing
a lot.

1 By John L. Rooke, Cottonwood.

I recall a story that is told of a Mr. Newman. He was a very scholarly gentleman from the South who spent some time in Florence, when that old camp was the principal town of the State. A mail route had recently been established from Lewiston to Florence, and the arrival of the mail was an event of some note. As the post office was in the general store, there was always a crowd waiting the arrival and distribution of the mail. One day when the mail arrived Mr. Newman was among the crowd that had gathered. As the stage driver brought the mail into the store, Mr. Newman jumped to his feet, jerked off his hat, and stood very straight and said, "Gentlemen, uncover in the presence of the United States Mail." Strange as it may seem, the whole crowd removed their hats and stood at attention while the man took the mail through the crowd into the little room that was used for a post office. Mr. Newman waited and received his mail, then went off down the street chuckling to himself.

As another example of the dry humor of the pioneer, I remember eating dinner with Mr. Frank Wyatt, the old cattleman, in White Bird when it was a real cow town. The food was excellent, the coffee was good even though it was a little stout for a young fellow, but Mr. Wyatt wanted his coffee so stout that it would float a wedge. He picked up his spoon and started slowly to stir his coffee. While he was stirring he said, "You know, for a small and delicate woman, the cook can hold a teakettle over a coffeepot longer than anybody I ever seen."

Billy the Bear

When Mike Rock was sheriff of Owyhee, he received word from a sheriff in Nevada to watch for one Billy the Bear, a dangerous criminal. "Be on guard," the sheriff wrote, "for Billy is quick on the trigger." That made Mike smile. If there was anyone in the world quicker on the trigger than he, then that was the man he wanted to meet; and he buckled his gun, jumped into his old model T and started out. His driving of his old car was enough to scare the daylights out of even a Billy. In early days, Mike had ridden a horse, giving rein and spurs and knowing he would get somewhere; and he drove a car on the same principle. He needed a road half a mile wide, for he zigzagged at top speed from right to left, from left to right, with his hand pressing the gas for all it was worth.

Perhaps Billy saw him coming crazily over the country when Mike entered the Strode Ranch in Oregon. With the Ford rattling at top speed and going as if dead drunk, Mike pulled into the yard and said he wanted some water for his radiator. He got a bucket and went to the kitchen; and there, with his back to him, stood Billy. But Billy did not turn. He was a dangerous man, all right, but he had heard of Mike Rock; and when Mike shoved a gun barrel into Billy's side, the outlaw did not reach for his irons. "Who are you?" he roared. "By God," said Mike, "I guess I'm the sheriff of Owyhee County." "You can't take me!" said Billy. "You're an Idaho sheriff and I'm in Oregon." "By hell," said Mike, "I'm no damned surveyor. I'm a sheriff and I'm still in Idaho so far as I'm concerned. So just stop your geography lesson and come along."

A Ragtime Requiem

The Chinese of Silver City in early days had everything but a brass band. In the winter of 1897-98, when the snow was very deep, one of the Chinese, a high Mason, died, and a very impressive funeral was planned. After much urging, the cornet player of the town band agreed to call his scattered musicians in; and when the day of burial came, the band was ready. When the procession reached Larson's Corner, the band was signaled to play a funeral march; but the members of the band, having no music with them, could think only of "There'll Be a Hot Time in the Old Town Tonight." For four blocks they played this melody for all they were worth. From the Samson livery barn to the cemetery, a distance of nearly three blocks, the snow was very deep, and the musicians plodded at a snail's pace.

As the casket was being lowered, the chief pallbearer ordered more music. The flabbergasted musicians considered; they didn't want to play an air that they had played for four blocks, so they broke into the popular melody, "Down Went McGinty." The Chinese were highly pleased. They gave the band boys a hundred dollars for their services, and thanked them profusely. They hadn't known what the tunes were anyway, and apparently assumed that they had listened to a funeral march and a requiem.

The Swede and His Corpse

A Swede in Silver City was known as Whistling Anderson because no matter where he went, walking or riding, he made the air ring with his melodies. He did more than that. He lived largely by his wits; and on one occasion his wits turned to a dead Chinese cook.

The cook died on Castle Creek, and Swede contracted for fifty dollars to deliver the dead man to Silver City. It was midwinter: Swede took the trail on skis. When he arrived at the Jordan place on Reynolds Creek, he learned that the dead man had been brought from Castle Creek and left lying on a porch, wrapped in an old piece of canvas. Upon finding him, Swede removed his skis and made a sled of them by using the frozen corpse, which he tied to them with leather thongs. Swede tied a tow rope to his sled and then put up for the night in Jordan's house.

Jordan liked practical jokes, too. He found an old poster from a mail-order house and tacked it on an outside wall of his cabin; he propped the corpse up under it; and then sent word to the Chinese of Silver City that he had a dead Chinaman on his premises. It was an excited bunch of Chinese who came pell-mell to the scene. Jordan pointed to the poster and declared that it was a sheriff's notice, to the effect that the corpse could not be removed without permission of the owner of the premises, and then only upon payment of a hundred dollars. Having a childlike belief that two thirds of the world was honest and the other third was dead, they paid the money and prepared for burial of the dead.

By this time Swede was awake again. He came out and grasped his tow rope and set off for the city, dragging the corpse and skis as a sled behind him. Upon reaching the summit of the mountain he had a downhill stretch to Booneville; whereupon, deciding that he might as well ride as walk, he sat on his sled and started down. All went well until he struck a curve in the trail; then Swede, corpse and all took to the air and went down the mountain like something out of a cannon. At the bottom, Swede dug himself out and seized his rope and set off again. When he reached Booneville his spirits were low and his distaste for dead Chinese almost overwhelming. Propping his dead man against the saloon, he went inside to renovate his temper.

He came out staggering and set off for Silver City, still dragging the dead man after him; and, miraculously enough, he arrived. But when he asked for payment, King Tan (alias Hog-Eye, alias Charlie) referred him to Lang who referred him to his cousin who referred him back to King Tan. Before the argument was finished, every Chinese person in Silver City was out to the graveyard where the imperturbable frozen corpse was still strapped to the skis. Then Swede lost his temper. "To hell with you all!" he cried. "Ay tank Ay tak him home and feed him to my pet fox!"—and at once started down the hill, dragging the dead fellow after him. Nothing is more superstitious than a superstitious Chinaman. With great lamentations they dug up fifty dollars and unfastened the dead fellow and propped him against a tombstone. They dug the ice out of his ears, the snow and frost out of his hair, and put a clean shirt on him; but the Swede was not interested in these sentimental doings. He had gone whistling into the city to fill his belly with whisky and food.

A Chinese Passes the Buck

Although the Chinese in early mining days gambled away their children in most cold-blooded fashion (one boy in Silver City, Little Ah Sid, changed hands at least ten times), they spared no pains in caring for their dead. They were so scrupulously attentive because they didn't want any spirits coming back to reproach or haunt them. While only the aristocrats, the brethren of the local Masonic order, were put underground to the music of orchestras and bands and loud wailing, even the lowliest were given careful burial.

One day a Chinese man died in a shack up the gulch and the undertaker was summoned to remove him. When he arrived at the shack he was astounded to hear a Chinese fellow shouting for all he was worth into the dead man's ear. He was almost out of his mind with woe and importunities and gesticulations, and continued for some minutes, kneeling and bellowing, while the flabbergasted undertaker watched him. Whereupon, apparently satisfied and at peace, the man rose and handed a dollar to another Chinese who had been silently waiting. Turning to the undertaker, the wailing one said: "Tlee-flo day ago beflo he die, I borra one dolla flom this dead flellow. Now I tella him I pay dolla to

this other flellow." And he smiled, happy in the knowledge
that if a ghost came back to stir up trouble, it would be the
other flellow's funeral and not his.

Plenty Clooked!

In the early days of Silver City a Chinese man died, and
to Facee, a well-known character about town, was given the
task of preparing the corpse for the undertaker. Facee,
though Chinese too, had never engaged in such work and
hardly knew what to do; but after deliberating he propped
the dead man against a wall and began to wash him, all
the while keeping up a monologue. His monologue became
steadily more excited because the corpse toppled every time
Facee turned to a washbasin to wring his cloth. After demanding, "Gee chly, wasa mala you? You clazy you no
stand up?" Facee lost his temper completely and socked the
dead man a terrific blow in his jaw. When he suddenly remembered that the deceased owed him three dollars, he
alternately propped him against the wall and swung at
him, and was thus busily engaged when Song Lee ran to
tell his countrymen of the desecration.

Song Lee came back up the hill at full speed, followed
by a half-dozen outraged Chinese, and yanked the corpse
away from Facee's indignant blows. There was violent
argument and almost a fight; but after a bit, Facee calmed
and gazed meditatively at the dead man whose face he had
fairly knocked out of shape. "All light," he said, "me no
care. Him no good. Him plenty clooked, plenty clooked!"

Potluck

The story was told by an early settler, now dead, that
her home was visited by several Indians who demanded
food. Though almost too terrified to move, she put a kettle
on the stove and added water and corn meal. After a bit
of cooking, the pot overflowed, whereupon she added the
overflow to another, and later to a third. The Indians were
amused by her frantic efforts to find enough pots to care
for the swelling meal; but nevertheless they sat and ate
gluttonously and went away. As they left they marked
a sign on the gatepost. The next day a band of Indians came
into the town and raided every house except the one with
the sign on the gate.

Ah Foo

Long ago in the little town of Cottonwood there lived a short Chinese man by the name of Ah Foo, who did not know how old he was or when he came to this country. After placer mining along Salmon River, he turned to odd jobs in Cottonwood and spent his spare time hunting for a buried treasure. He had heard some Chinese from Florence had

Ah Foo

set out for Walla Walla with a pile of gold dust but had buried their treasure in a gum boot for safety and had died before recovering it. Ah Foo never found it. In his extreme old age he became blind, and his white friends cared for him until he went into senile dementia and was placed in the asylum at Orofino.

Bear Pete

Many are the stories told today about an old-timer who was known far and wide as Bear Pete. The following is typical. One day while Pete was riding through the wilderness he met an Indian who asked for whisky. Pete refused, whereupon the Indian offered him for a pint his pack pony, saddle pony, and all his equipment. At this point in his tale Pete always paused. When asked, "Well, did you trade?" he answered: "You darn tootun I didn't. That was the only pint I had. But it does kinda go to show that an Injun likes his whisky."

Sleepy Can

Sleepy Can was something of a problem to the community. He was so poor, so bedraggled and forlorn that he fairly broke the hearts of all the townspeople who watched him as he shuffled along the streets. You would think to look at him that he had never had a dollar in his life. Apparently, he had no food at all and very little in the way of clothes. The weather was such that he could not get through the winter in such pitiful plight; so the townspeople decided there was nothing to do but send him to the poorhouse. Sleepy fought like a wild cat; he didn't want to go; he chattered and wailed every step of the way and after they got him there he kept running out; so they finally burned his clothes (the few he had on his back) and that was a catastrophe, for Sleepy had eight hundred dollars in bills tucked away in his pants. After that, he simply wilted away, and it wasn't long until he died.

The Meanest Man in Idaho

Bert Churchill went into the Salmon River country after the days of the mining boom. He built the trail from Dixie over the mountain that bears his name, and down into the stupendous chasm which forms the course of the Salmon River through central Idaho. There on the north side of the stream, about halfway between the Middle Fork and the South Fork, he settled on one of the narrow bars of fertile land occasionally found between the canyon wall and the river.

Like most hillbillies, Churchill was an independent and self-sustaining individual, but in two respects he was unlike the majority of "nesters" among the high hills—he had only one hand and he had a wife. Furthermore, he wasn't very kind to his wife, although he was probably fair enough to most people during the many years they lived in that untamed country.

One day early in summer when the river was a swirling torrent created by melting snows, Churchill, in company with two other men, was making his way down the stream in a rowboat. At flood season the river carries much driftwood, including uprooted trees, sometimes of gigantic proportions. The boat, in an effort to avoid one of these, was caught crosswise with the current and capsized.

The Meanest
Man in Idaho

The three men were swept down toward the foaming cascade known as Richardson's Rapids. They were all powerful swimmers. But how feeble seemed the efforts of mere man against such a torrent of wild water! However, they succeeded in using the current to help them toward a high boulder near the middle of the stream above the rapids. They were able to clamber upon the top of this rock where they clung—wet and shivering—through the night.

The next morning they were discovered. A rescue was brought about by throwing a long lariat rope from the bank to the rock, where two of the men in turn caught it, plunged into the icy flood, and were drawn to safety.

Only Churchill remained on the rock. The rope was thrown to him. But instead of putting it around his body as the others had done, he grasped it in his hand and with the metal hook which served him for the other hand. The hook was fastened in a leather and metal cap fitted over the stump of his arm and secured to his body by a leather harness passing around his shoulders. When the mighty force of the current struck him, this harness, weakened by much wear, snapped under the strain, and unable to retain his grip with the other hand he was swept down by the turgid flood.

He struggled feebly and hopelessly as the rushing waters carried him on toward the roaring rapids. As it became evident that he could never survive, his wife, watching from the bank, clapped her hands and exclaimed fervently, "Good! there goes the meanest man in Idaho!"

This tale is still told by the natives along the Salmon River.

Idaho Joke Book

This story is sworn to as actual fact by many persons still living. In the Mountain Home area, a young man and his bride moved into a cabin which he had built and went to bed. Later, hearing a strange sound, yet unable to see anything in the gloom, he left the bed to investigate and was at once struck by several rattlesnakes. Crying to his bride to draw the quilts over her and not leave the bed for any reason, he sank to the floor and died there, with snakes ankle-deep around him. The girl did not leave the bed and was discovered later by friends. It was then learned that the young man had built his fireplace over a nest of rattlers, and the warmth of the fire had drawn them to the earth floor of the cabin.

A letter was delivered to Cornelius Sprawels of Silver City with this address on the envelope:

> Cornelius Sprawels, the web-foot scrub
> To whom this letter wants to go,
> Cutting cordwood for his grub
> In Silver City, Idaho.

According to the *Idaho World*, June 3, 1865, stiff hair indicates obstinacy; sleek hair, patience; curly locks, wit and love of pleasure; baldness, an active mind, unless the man brushes his hair in an attempt to cover the bald spot; to do so declares a mean and vulgar spirit. If he wears a wig, he is a trickster. Premature grayness perhaps indicates a dissolute life.

A white cow was killed by a railway engine; and when the man who owned her asked for damages he received a letter from the railroad company which said: "We cannot pay. A white cow cannot be seen very well by the engineer." To that the man retorted: "What am I to do? Do I have to go out and paint all my cows?" The company paid.

In the seventies on Camas Prairie, farmers got only thirty or forty cents a bushel for grain, and could not afford to ship hogs; so they decided to drive the beasts to markets in Montana, Oregon, and Utah. They learned, however, that the feet of hogs got raw and bleeding on the long march; whereupon it was decided to shoe them. This was done by covering the feet with pitch and then letting the beast wade around in loose sand. Later, warm tar was used; and thus shod, the hogs were driven to the slaughtering pens.

During the boom days of Nicholia, two beeves were killed each day at the slaughter pens. Hungry Lemhi Indians would stand near and grab the intestines as they were thrown out and suck them dry.

From the *Idaho World*, Oct. 23, 1885: Wm. Horton tells
a fish story: The first mess of trout we caught from the
Grosventre River were filled with grit. None of the boys
could explain it. Jo Voshay said to me, "Don't you remember the remark I made when I showed you the trout?" "About
their yellow color?" "Yes." I went out and caught a few
more and examined them closely. I found gold stowed away
all around the gills and got a good prospect by making a
thorough clean-up. I got more by scraping the trout, for
some way or another the gold had got under and on top
of the scales. We made good wages cleaning up the trout.
The average was about four-bits a fish.

In early days, a bigshot from the East was expected to
arrive on the stage to visit a mine in which he was interested; and the natives decided the visitor was important
enough to be worth a high-falutin reception. So the band
was ordered out and everyone dressed in his Sunday clothes,
and they all started for the mining town of Dewey to greet
the lordly one from the East. When the stage drew in, the
band began to play, "Hail, the Conquering Hero Comes!"
and a citizen stepped forth to deliver the address of welcome.
Then the stage door was opened and out stepped the one and
only passenger, a small, much-confused and half-scared-out-
of-his-wits Chinaman.

Mrs. D. T. Babb, of Lewiston, reports that a woman,
now dead, watched as a child the Rev. Henry Spalding marry
a couple of Indians. When the buck told Spalding he already
had a wife, the minister said it was not right to have two
wives. The Indian was thoughtful for a long moment before
answering, "All right, me kill one."

Hans Bierbauer was up before the justice of the peace,
charged with habitual drunkenness. As he upbraided Hans,
the judge's voice rocked with emotion. "Miserable creature
that you are, six times within the last month you have been
here before me! Drink has drowned in you all sense of
shame—made you insensible not only to disgrace but to all
human feeling. Your children are branded with the stigma
of a drunkard's name, and starved because of a drunkard's

vice. Rum shows itself in your shaking limbs and in your bleared and watery eyes. It has made your nose—" "Chudge," the old toper interjected, "don't you call no names to my nose. Dot is a gut respectable nose. Don't you see dot it blushes in shame for the rest of me?"

--

The Big Eddy Saloon in early Boise stood where the Ada Theater now stands. Run by Joe Kinney, it was known as the loudest and toughest spot in the town. The story is told of how one man was killed and several injured in a free-for-all brawl when the fighters collided with the ice chest which somehow was connected with the ceiling. As it upset, the huge chest brought most of the ceiling down with it. The debris practically buried a dozen furious fellows who were punching away with all their might.

--

The *Idaho World* wrote Sept. 12, 1879: Quite a curiosity was found a few days ago near the camp of the workmen on the new toll road near Yankee Fork. It is a mountain ram's head deeply imbedded in a pine tree about six feet from the ground. The right horn is outside and curls partly around the tree, while the front of the skull and most of the left horn are covered with a growth of wood. The tree is a thrifty pine fifteen inches in diameter. How the ram's head came there will perhaps remain a mystery to scientists, but men of the mountains, familiar with the fighting propensities of the wild buck, can easily explain it. The ram, whose head is now a part of the tree, stood near what was then a pine sapling. When he made a rush at ram No. 2, the latter jumped aside and the old warrior's head, coming in contact with the small tree, split it, and one of his horns was caught in the cleft; and unable to free himself, he was held there at the mercy of his foe. The rest is easily guessed. He was butted to death and eaten by wild animals.

--

Jim Helmsworth worked at the Rossland mine. While hoisting a bucket of ore from the bottom of a hundred-foot shaft, with two miners at the shaft's bottom, Jim saw the crank of the windlass break and the bucket of ore begin a swift descent to the bottom. Jim, it is said, did not hesitate an instant. He thrust his arm against the cogs of the wheel,

Big Eddy
Saloon

and the cogs ground the flesh and bone of his arm into a pulp clear to his shoulder. But the bucket was stopped and the lives of the two men in the shaft were saved.[1]

When Indians up north received money for their lands, they all rushed to Spokane to buy buggies, wagons, and whatnots. By the time the big chief arrived, however, there wasn't a carriage left; so he bought a hearse and loaded his family into it and returned home. His carriage for many years was the envy of every Indian on the reservation.

In early times in Lewiston, "at home" day was formally observed by the women. Calls were made in the morning; a siesta was taken in the afternoon. A Yankee woman, with rugs and cushions out on the line, wanted to know of her neighbor how she could afford so much time for running around to visit. She received this reply: "Perhaps if you'd take more of it you might have that 'fillin'' your husband admires in other women so much." By fillin', the lady meant adorable curves.

Many persons still living swear that this story is true. In Mountain Home once lived a butcher who was cockeyed. He killed his beasts by knocking them on the head with an axe and then sticking them with a knife; and one day he took an assistant out to help him butcher the calf. After the animal was caught, the assistant held it and the butcher raised his axe; whereupon the assistant yelled wildly, "Hey, in the name of God, you gonna hit where you're looking?" "Sure," said the butcher. "That's what I aim to do." "Then, by hell, you'd better hold the calf!"

Two prospectors, eating lunch, saw a bear and her two cubs coming around a bluff and toward them. As the mother passed, with the cubs trailing, one of the men whistled and the cubs stopped and looked curiously all around them. The old bear, seeing them pause, grunted ominously and the cubs resumed their journey; but when a man whistled again, the rear cub stopped and looked, and

---

1 Coeur d'Alene *Press*, Golden Anniversary Edition, July, 1937.

"Hey, you gonna hit where you're looking?"

repeated the experience every time the whistling sounded. Whereupon, the mother, annoyed, turned about and approached the offending cub and gave him such a box on his ear that he was knocked squealing into the grass and thicket. The old bear went on again and the cub dutifully followed; nor could the whistling of both men make him pause or look aside.

A story is told of Bill Borden of the Buffalo Hump country who, having much money (he was a relative of the milk Borden) paid any old-timer ten dollars a day to drink with him when he visited Boise. Bill always soaked away more than he could carry and was thrown into jail; and after two or three such experiences, he bought the nicest bedroom set in the city and had it installed in his cell. Thereafter, before coming to Boise to engage in a drinking bout, he always wired the jail to reserve his cell for him.

A Circle C Ranch cowboy encountered a bear in the mountains when he had no gun, but he did have his lariat. Riding above the bear, he chased the beast downhill; and because a bear tumbles and rolls frightfully on a downgrade, he was able to overtake and rope it. Thereupon he threw

Making
'Em Mind

the free end of the rope over a stout limb, seized it and wrapped it three times around his saddle horn, and then drew the beast into the air and held him suspended. Another cowboy came on the scene and was sent for a gun; and meanwhile both pony and rider applied all their weight. to keep the bear dangling and roaring, with only his hind feet barely touching earth.

The *Idaho World* for Oct. 13, 1866, reported that Pat Mahaffey came home the worse for liquor. Turning sick, he sat by the stove and vomited into a box in which his wife had placed several goslings. After a bit, Pat looked down and saw them and roared: "God a'mighty, wife, when did I swaller them things?"

When the first funeral was held in Pocatello, there was neither Bible nor minister in the town; but Charlie Napper, a saloonkeeper, went ahead with the ceremony. The dead man was buried close by the Portneuf River, though the grave for some reason was not filled; and upon leaving, Charlie looked back and saw a man crawling out of it. "Hey, you!" he shouted. "Get back in there and mind your business!" That night the river rose under heavy rains and water filled the grave, with the consequence that the coffin rose to the land surface and floated. In disgust, Charlie yanked it out and buried it again on a hill above high water.

An old-timer near Hazelton was shot through the throat by a brigand and thereafter had to take his nourishment through a funnel into his neck. Persons still tell of the

The Perambulating Skull.

picture he made, month after month and year after year, when he poured whisky into the funnel and waited expectantly until it reached his stomach and then blinked his eyes with quiet satisfaction.

~~

From the *Idaho World,* July 4, 1878: While out looking for an errant cow late Saturday night, Len Atkins saw by the light of his lantern a human skull bouncing along the path before him. Len is no coward but he admits that his hair stood on end. It came toward him, twisting, rolling over and over, dancing crazily up and down. From his place of concealment, he watched the progress of this macabre performance which continued along the same erratic lines until it reached a colony of prairie dogs where suddenly it came to a rest. A score of chattering dogs came out of their holes, and the head of another dog emerged from the cavity of the skull, followed presently by its body. There is an ancient Indian burial ground in this vicinity. Whether the animal was caught in the skull or used it as a vehicle to return home cannot be said.

~~

A bunch of miners came to town for the day and celebrated for all they were worth. After they had done all the saloons, they headed for home, but one of them, less certain on his feet, wandered away and got lost. Deciding to call it a day anyhow, he lay down to sleep, not knowing he was in a graveyard. Upon awakening the next morning with rain in his face, he sat up and looked around him and exclaimed: "Resurrection, be God, and me the first bloody bugger awake!"

~~

In early times, the only passenger on a stagecoach threw open the door, leaped to the ground, sprinted across a yard, and stood on his head with his heels against a wall. When asked what the matter was, the man righted himself and said: "Well, standun on my head is the only position I ain't been in on that whoop-danged stagecoach; so I decided to do a full program."

~~

In the Idaho *Statesman* for May 15, 1866, an announcement said: There is a letter in the Boise City postoffice directed to Mr. Wm. Johnson, Boyse River, Idaho, Oregon,

Colorado Territory. Some indignant mail clerk has endorsed on it, "If you know where this letter belongs, for God's sake send it."

The booming early town of Thunder City felt its oats. The official description of it declared that it was bounded on the north by the Aurora Borealis, on the east by the rising sun, on the south by the vernal equinox, and on the west by the Day of Judgment.

The following advertisement appeared in the *Idaho World,* Sept. 30, 1892: Notice is hereby given that if you will come to my store three times a day during the next year and purchase a drink of whisky each time, paying me ten cents a drink, at the end of the year I will donate for the benefit of your family: 5 barrels of my best flour; 100 pounds fine granulated sugar; 100 pounds of rice; 50 pounds coffee; 10 gallons syrup; 50 yards muslin; 60 yards calico; 3 prs. shoes; a $10.50 cloak for your wife; and then I will have $25 left to pay for the liquor you drink. J. Mickel Merch, Prohibition Advance Advocate.

Many Chinese who came to Idaho mining towns were addicted to opium and often had the drug sent under false labels. In wintertime the mail was often carried afoot. In 1893 Jack Anderson was carrying mail from Mt. Idaho and had in his cargo several tins that bore tobacco labels. As he trudged along mile after mile, the sharp edges of the tins lacerated his shoulders; and after eating his supper the first night, he resolved to flatten the tins out a bit, and so laid into his mail pouch with a large club. After pounding away at the sharp corners, he became suspicious and peered into the pouch and saw sticky opium oozing from the tins and spreading over the mail. This discovery marked the end of the delivery into Elk City of opium by carriers.

Many years ago, a group of persons was traveling in southeastern Idaho and camped for the night. In the morning a woman laid her six-weeks' baby on a pallet in the sun, and was horrified a few minutes later to discover that it was gone. Then someone remembered having seen an eagle circling over the camp, and at once a search was undertaken. When the nest was found, the fierce female eagle refused to budge, and one of the men shot the creature and threw her off the nest. And there, a little scratched but not seriously hurt, was the baby among a half-dozen baby eagles.

An old-timer in Kootenai Valley says that formerly there was a homesteader in the area whose housekeeping ways were always open to suspicion. The man had a dog which he called Two Waters, and not until after the hound's death could he be prevailed upon to explain why he called a beast so unusual a name. Then the truth came out. When visitors had complained that the dishes and cooking utensils were not very clean, the old fellow had always answered: "They're as plumb clean as Two Waters can get them."

The *Idaho World* for Nov. 4, 1879, recorded the suicide of Tom Kearnan, of Challis. The weapon used was a pistol; the ball passed through his brain. Tom left a note saying simply, "I want to get there before all the best claims are taken up."

In 1862 a Washington territorial judge, under commission of President Lincoln, held at Pierce City the first term of court there. His grand jury returned an indictment of Lincoln for murder, apparently a mirthful exhibition of bravado on the part of his honor, the judge. Though there is no record of the proceedings, the indictment has been well authenticated.

A Coeur d'Alene Indian, wishing to comply with the intricacies of civilization, proved himself so industrious a member of the community that the local bank lent him money, taking twenty-two ponies as collateral. When the money was due the Indian paid it. The banker, observing that he still had cash, tried to persuade him to deposit it in the bank, explaining to him the advantages. The Indian thereupon laid his money on the desk and asked: "How many ponies you?"

This advertisement appeared in the *Idaho World* for Oct. 13, 1866: Lost or strade from the subscriber a sheep all over white, one leg was black and half his body. All persons shall receive five dollars to bring him. He was a she goat.

Many a man formerly, as well as today, drank more than he could carry. One of them staggered home late in an afternoon and learned that his wife and daughters were entertaining guests. As he entered, he heard one of his daughters say that she had washed her hair and was unable to do much with it. That gave him an idea and he grinned. "Egscuse, ladish, pleaz egscuse. I've jist washt my feet and I jist can't do anything with them."

About thirty years ago, the time arrived for some placer mining Chinese to dig up their dead and ship them to China. Two boys, watching them exhume, waited until everyone had left the cemetery and then seized the best looking casket and managed to get it to a near-by creek. They repaired it as best they could and used it all summer for a fishing boat.

Charles Wells raised two steers for oxen, and when they were grown he set out to break them. He hitched one to the top of a fallen tree, thinking that if the animal ran, the branches would gouge into the earth and stop him. The beast ran all right, and before Charlie could get out of the way; and after he was knocked down, rolled under the limbs, and at last delivered at the rear end, he sat up to discover that he hadn't a stitch of clothing left on him except one sock.

This happened on the Snake River bottomlands close to American Falls. Two cowboys were riding herd one day and got pretty drunk. They lay around for several days, drinking and wondering where their cattle were; and slept in blankets on the ground. One of the cowboys, awakened by a noise, sat up and saw a rattlesnake, coiled and ready to spring. He grinned (or says he did) and cried: "Strike, durn you, strike, and see which one of us gets hurt the worst!" The snake struck and died.

The many caves on the face of Squaw Butte, five miles north of Emmett, are infested with rattlesnakes. Many years ago, two lost hunters, overtaken by night and storm, crawled into one of the caves facing eastward and fell asleep. In the morning they awakened to find themselves literally covered with snakes that had coiled around and about them to share their warmth. They dared not move or even speak; and for more than two hours they lay quietly, hardly breathing, and wondering how they could get out of there. The sun saved them. When it rose and shone warmly into the cave, one by one the snakes crawled away.

In the mining town of Wardner, three men worked to accumulate a fortune, two of whom were generous of heart, and one miserly. When one of the generous fellows died, the other two grieved at his funeral and laid a huge floral offering on his casket; whereupon, feeling that they should do more for one whom they had both loved, the generous one suggested that each should put a hundred dollars on the coffin before it was laid away, and forthwith deposited his hundred in currency. The other said it was splendid idea; whereupon he wrote a check for two hundred and put it on the coffin, and took the hundred in currency as his rightful change.

This story is sworn to by members of the Albion Normal School. In May, 1882, a stage driver, running between Albion and Kelton, Utah, discovered in Kelton that he had no whip. There were no trees or willows in that desolate area; but on the station platform he saw a poplar sapling of the size he needed, and this he used. How many times he laid it upon his weary beasts in that long drive, nobody knows, but when he arrived, the sapling was frayed and worn. Nevertheless, he planted it, hardly expecting it to grow; and today it is a magnificent poplar on the John Parke homestead, two miles southwest of Albion.

The *Idaho World* of Aug. 4, 1876, reports that William Horton, Macon Smith, and Tom Barry were on a hunting trip in the Hagerman area when they saw the strangest sight they had ever seen. Hundreds of hoop snakes had taken their tails in their mouths and were rolling down the canyon wall to the river where they unrolled themselves and slid to the edge and drank. Horton reported to the editor that: "This species of snake thickens itself a little in front of its point of contact with the earth so as to make itself heavier at this spot than in any other part of its body. As the center of gravity falls in front of the base, the snake revolves in the direction of its 'wad.' "

~~

Two old prospectors, living alone in the hills, quarreled as lonely persons do and one shot the other dead. He went to town and reported to the sheriff; and the sheriff sent a deputy, Ed Winn, and a doctor named Bean from Caribou to the cabin in the hills. Upon arriving there, they wondered how to freight the dead body out, inasmuch as they had only the horses they had ridden; and Bean proposed that they cut the head off. This they did and took it with them. Upon their return, however, no one know what to do with the head. It was kicked around from place to place and at last came to rest in a saloon where men jested over it as they drank. Then it disappeared and nobody knows where it went to, though some say it was preserved in alcohol. The practice of cutting off a dead man's head when it was impossible to fetch him out of the mountains was not an uncommon one in early days.

~~

One day a young sheepman, Henry Lane, was traveling from Richfield to the hills when he ran over a dog. Seeing that it was mortally wounded, he shot it; and observing further that it was fat and sleek, he smiled ironically and skinned it out and took the meat to Carey and sold it to a Chinese for mutton. This much of the story is well authenticated. The addition may be apocryphal; for it is said that the young man stopped to eat at the Chinese restaurant a day or two later and learned that he had been served dog, though the Chinese still believed it was mutton and said it was velly fine.

~~

In the *Idaho World*, of Oct. 31, 1879, a man tells this story of his cow. Observing that she gave less and less milk, he followed her to the hillside where she grazed and there found a snake that looked to him as big as a fence post. He put the cow in the barn for several days; but upon releasing her, she failed to return. He found her where he had found her before, milked dry, and with the snake beside her. "That," the man reported, "is a strange instance of affection between a cow and a snake."

My grandfather's sister came across the plains in a covered wagon. She had to sleep on the ground. One cold night, after a wet snow, she awoke to find that her long hair was frozen to the earth. My grandfather had to fetch an axe and chop her hair loose.[1]

A pioneer in the Caldwell area set out to butcher hogs at his neighbor's for winter meat, and after the slaughter was done, he loaded ten of the beasts into his wagon and started home. After driving for an hour, he and his son were attacked by wolves, with the starved creatures coming from behind and smelling the meat and leaping at the wagon. With an axe, the man was able to fend off one, but not two or three together; and he decided, therefore, that he would have to throw flesh to them. Hog by hog he fed the wolves as his son journeyed through the night. When he reached home, he had three and a half hogs of the ten he had started with.

Not many Idahoans of the past have more stories told about them than that strange person of the South Fork area of the Boise River who has passed into legend as Johnny-behind-the-rock. He came to Idaho from England and with earnest but scrupulous methods accumulated a great fortune. Discovering that his friends as well as his enemies were bent on getting his money, he moved in disgust with all his money and belongings and lived in a crude dugout behind a huge rock, spending the rest of his years there in his hermitage and guarding his gold. Much more apocryphal is the story that he moved because of disgust for the cleanliness of his wife and sought a home where he could have a dirt floor and plenty of filth.

A wealthy Easterner came to Idaho after a moose. He had never heard of buck fever or buck "ager," that uncontrollable nervousness which seizes the greenhorn at the critical moment, and perhaps has never heard of it yet. With an old-timer as a guide, he set out; but when, looking across a clearing, he saw a huge bull moose staring at him, his eyes became as big as saucers; and instead of firing, he worked his rifle until he had emptied it of every shell. Ob-

---

1 Bernice Blakely.

serving what he did, the guide fired and dropped the beast; whereupon the Easterner threw his rifle and his hat in the air and yelled, "I got him!" and went off at full speed toward the fallen animal. He thought he had fired. He thought it was he who had killed the moose, and nothing under heaven could convince him he had not. Today he has the mounted head in his home and tells visitors how he dropped the big bull at the first shot.

~

Years ago a tramp was making his devious way along the Boise road when he conceived a brilliant idea for raising the wind. He knew that the Wells, Fargo stage would pass along the road in about half an hour so he took off his coat, tore his shirt and pockets, rolled in the dust, and managed to tie himself after a good deal of difficulty all too well to a tree.

His intention was to tell the stage passengers that he had been foully dealt with by road agents, thinking they would make up a purse to repair his losses. The stage, however, took a short cut by a new road that day and didn't pass him. After waiting until dusk, he tried to free himself of his bonds but before he succeeded in doing this, a grizzly came down out of the mountains and picnicked off the greater part of his left leg.[1]

~

In early days, two men were lost in the central Idaho desert and had nothing to eat for several days except the flesh of stray dogs. One day, one of them fell to his knees and started barking like a hound; and his partner, seeing him, thought the man had suddenly gone out of his mind. He was wondering whether to flee or bash the fellow in the head with a lava rock when he observed that his partner was trying his best to draw within reach a dog that was standing over the ridge by an isolated Indian tepee.

~

According to the *Idaho World*, old Mose came to Boise from the Banner mine and went into a restaurant, seeking a huge dinner. He yelled for a waiter and said he wanted a square meal; whereupon the waiter skipped briskly away and returned with a neatly bound bill of fare which he

[1] *Idaho World*, Nov. 22, 1878.

opened and laid before Mose. Mose stared at it and then shoved it away and roared: "Don't try to cram any book-larnun down me, young feller! Grub's what I want! *Grub* —and damn quick too!"

━━

A notoriously lazy man in the Coeur d'Alene country failed to comply with requirements in proving up on his homestead. At the land office, when asked what improvements he had, he said he had a jug out with a shingle on it. The recorder, thinking the fellow had a foreign accent or an inflamed tooth, listed the improvement as a dugout with a shingled roof. Later, when the claim was contested and the lazy one was in a fair way to be tried for perjury, an investigator found in a sheltered spot a jug with a shingle tied upon it for a roof.

━━

The *Idaho World* for April 28, 1866, declared: It is said that if one always sleeps with his head to the north, one will live to a ripe old age, for in that position the iron in the body becomes magnetized and this increases the energy of the vital principle of the system.

━━

In 1865 the *Idaho World* announced: We are authorized to offer a reward of two dollars and a half in clean gold dust for positive information as to who *is* Governor of Idaho.

━━

The *Avalanche* in Silver City reported under July 16, 1870, that the chairman of a committee of vigilantes had taken an obnoxious person to duck him in cold water. The chairman said: "We took the thief down to the river, made a hole in the ice and proceeded to duck him—but he slipped out of our hands and hid under the ice; and as he has been there over eight hours now it is supposed he is drowned."

━━

A Clark County farmer swears that this story is true. He took a cow to Idaho Falls to have her sold at auction; but after hearing the auctioneer describe her qualities, the amount of milk she gave, her fine calves and the number of them, and the small amount of food she ate for her size, he grew excited and bid on her himself. She was sold to him.

Soon after the lumber camp at Clarkia came into existence, a lumberjack fell out of a tree and broke his neck. The body was taken to Fernwood, the sheriff notified; but instead of going to the scene himself, the sheriff sent the justice of the peace, who carried with him a book containing every record in the county. He crawled upon the wagon and pulled the quilt back from the man's face and said, "The statute says when a man is dead to bury him. I now pronounce you dead."

The soil in the cemetery overlay granite, and the gravediggers, upon running into rock, sent for dynamite and whisky. Alternately they drank and blasted, and sent for more whisky and dynamite; and by the time the hole was large enough for the coffin, the diggers were hilariously happy. As the casket was being lowered, a big Irishman fell, unseen by his companions, into the hole under the box, and the coffin was lowered upon him. He made all kinds of queer noises, but amid his bellows and yells and curses he said quite clearly, "Take it off!" With their hair standing on end (for the other men thought it was the corpse yelling), the diggers turned and fled, and tore down thirty yards of cemetery fence in their haste to escape. The Irishman finally crawled out and cursed furiously until he found the whisky jug; whereupon he sat upon the grave and finished it.

A huge rambling house in the Salmon River country is entirely shingled with milk cans.

An old-time prospector always put on a dozen eggs to boil for breakfast, knowing that he would be lucky to find a good one among them.

A woman in the mining town of Nicholia used to tell of hard times when a soupbone was passed from family to family, with each taking from it as much nourishment as he could.

Tendoy, chief of the Lemhi tribe, had fifty wives. Some Christian snoops thought it scandalous and reported the matter to a State senator who spoke to Tendoy about it.

"See here, Tendoy, you pick out your favorite squaw and tell the others to skin out." Tendoy grinned. "You tell 'em," he said.

＊

Senator Jim Dyer always left his door unlocked so that hungry passersby could go in and cook themselves a meal. Never was anything stolen except his sourdough, in which he took special pride; whereupon he bought a new slop jar and put his dough in it and set the jar under his bed. It was not stolen again.

＊

The story is told of an early Idaho town (nameless here) which one day incorporated and looked around to see what it did not have that an incorporated place should have. It had no cemetery because nobody there had ever died; whereupon a public-spirited committee sailed out and shot a fellow of dubious reputation and used him to get the cemetery going.

＊

The chief store in the early days of Fernwood was called a poolhall, but in reality was a store, with a saloon at the rear. Periodically this store was robbed. One night, when the owner was preparing to leave, two men entered and demanded hands up, one of the men approaching the owner, the other remaining in the doorway. Instead of obeying, the owner dropped the cash box to the floor and dived under the counter for his gun. The bandit leaned over the counter and shot him, the bullet striking the side of his face and shattering the jaw and knocking out several teeth. Staggering to his feet and grasping the counter, the owner cried, "All right, you coward, kill me if that is what you want to do! You don't give a man the smallest chance so you might as well finish the job." The bandit began to curse but was arrested by a voice which said: "Come on, you've done enough damage for one night." These words were spoken by his companion who had been guarding the door.

＊

The *Idaho World* for Sept. 3, 1865, reported that a disappointed vigilante said that the "vigilance movement would have been successful if we had not been foolish enough to admit two or three Democrats into the organization."

*You
Tell 'Em*

A Nez Perce Indian approached the cabin of a pioneer and asked for food. The settler dismissed him. When the Indian insisted that he could smell food, he was told to get along and lose no time about it. Many years later, a footsore traveler stopped at the home of an Indian and asked if he could borrow a horse to continue his journey. His own horse, he said, had broken a leg. "I got no horse," said the Indian. "But I can see horses." "One day long time ago," said the Indian, "I could smell food and you told me to smell it. Now you look at my horses."

The *Idaho World* of Dec. 10, 1864, reported: On Dec. 8th, Mrs. O. Flannigan gave birth to her eighteenth child. Mr. Flannigan is as well as could be expected.

In the Malad Valley, many years ago, a Millerite predicted the end of the world. So many persons believed him that a huge crowd gathered upon a hill top and awaited the end of the earth and sky. An elderly woman, long of chin and skeptical of faith, wearied of the hot sun, climbed to the top of a stack of hay to rest. She fell asleep. Deciding that the world would continue, some men set the stack of hay afire as a joke; and when the flames had circled it and smoke was billowing skyward, the awakened woman leapt to her feet in great excitement. "Just my luck!" she yelled. "In hell, just like I expected!"[1]

Bears love perfume. If some is sprayed on a rock or a stump, they will play around it for hours.

A farmer who distrusted and sometimes despised lawyers went to one to tell a tale of woe. "My fences is good," he said. "I keep them up. But cattle just busts in here and there and yonder. And there ain't no better fence in the valley." "Give me the case," said the lawyer. "I'll prosecute. I'll stop it." "Yes, but could you, Mr. Jones? Anyway, dang it, the cattle are mine."

An old-timer is said to have chopped the tail off his cat so the door would not remain open so long in cold weather

---

[1] From the unpublished reminiscences of Alexander Toponce of Malad.

while the cat was entering the house. Another, facing starvation, cut off his cat's tail and boiled it and ate the meat; and the cat itself gnawed for an hour on the bone.

A rancher in Nicholia had a black cow that he kept alive during a hard winter by feeding her on boiled badgers and her own milk. She could "pick a bone cleaner than a dog could." After she learned to suck herself, she had to be muzzled; but she did not suck herself after her calf came.

In the Malad Valley, an old Welsh woman was told that it was good to confess her sins and get the matter off her conscience. It was explained to her, further, that she ought to confess in public meeting for the salutary effect on others as well as on herself. "Then everyone will forgive and forget." "Well, me," she said, "now I'm always willun to forgive and forget but I'll always remember."

The stage, while journeying from Fairview to Silver City, was stopped half way up the mountain by a terrific blizzard. The only passenger was a Chinese woman, and both she and the driver were nearly frozen to death before the latter could think of a way out. He made a hole in a snowbank and stored her there and set out for help. Upon returning, he could not for the life of him tell where he had left the passenger, for falling snow had made a smooth surface of the entire area around the coach. With a shovel he started to dig, and after laboring for an hour without success he began to strike into the deep snow with the shovel blade in an attempt to find her. After delivering one of his blows he was almost paralyzed by an ear-splitting shriek. In the next moment the astonished woman came up out of her cold white bed; but although she was bleeding a little she was not seriously injured.

An editor of the *Boise News* in 1871 was alarmed by the number of murders wherein women were given as the principal cause, and declared that he was turning over a new social leaf, saying: All men's wives who have hitherto enjoyed the advantage of our acquaintance are hereby notified that this ceases today, never to be renewed. Men perish ingloriously every day for being on speaking terms with married women, and we're not waiting for our turn. Deeply grateful for the past forbearance of aggrieved husbands, we make our bow and retire. Whoever shall attempt to introduce us to his wife, or to any other man's wife, will be regarded as conspiring against our life and will thus be denounced in the columns of this paper.

⁓

The following recipe for making a fashionable woman is from the *Idaho World* of April 25, 1872:

Take ninety pounds of flesh and bone, mainly bones, wash clean and bore holes in the ears, bend the neck to conform with the Grecian bend, the Boston dip, the kangaroo droop, the Saratoga slope or the bullfrog beak, as the taste inclines. Then add three yards of linen, one hundred yards of ruffles and seventy-five yards of edging, eighteen yards of dimity, one pair silk-cotton hose with patent hip attachments, one pair of false calves, six yards of flannel, embroidered, one pair Balmoral boots with heels three inches high, four pounds whalebone in strips, seventeen hundred and sixty yards of steel wire, three-quarters of a mile of tape, ten pounds of raw cotton or two wire hemispheres, one wire basket that would hold a bushel, four copies of the World, one hundred and fifty yards of silk or other dress goods, five hundred yards of lace, fourteen hundred yards fringe and other trimmings, twelve gross of buttons, one box pearl face powder, one saucer of carmine and an old hare's foot, one bushel of false hair frizzed and fretted *à la maniaque,* one bundle Japanese switches with rats, mice and other varmints, one peck of hairpins, one lace handkerchief, nine inches square, with patent holder. Perfume with attar of roses or "Blessed Baby" or "West End." Stuff the head with fashionable novels, ball tickets, playbills, wedding-cards, some scandal, a lot of wasted time and a very little sage. Add a half-grain of common sense, three scruples of religion and a modicum of modesty. Season with vanity, affectation and folly. Garnish with earrings, finger rings, breastpins, chains, bracelets, feathers and flowers to suit the taste. Pearls and diamonds may be added and pinchbeck from the dollar-store will do.

Whirl all around in a fashionable circle and stew by gaslight for six hours.

This dish is highly ornamental, a *pièce de résistance* for the head of your table upon grand occasions but, being somewhat indigestible and highly expensive, is not commended for daily consumption in the home.

～

In early times, a man named John was something of a horse trader, and now and then shipped a carload to Denver. He did not always ship horses that belonged to him, and one day was hailed into court to explain how he came into possession of a certain beast. "I didn't," he said, looking the judge straight in the eye. "It was this way. I was riding along through the brush and I saw a long rope and I picked it up. It had a horse on the end of it." "But you didn't know that when you picked up the rope?" "I didn't know it. I just found a rope and took it along with me." "The case is dismissed," said the judge.

～

A man named Jordon lived long ago on Reynolds Creek. To pay for the cost of a stretch of road, he erected a toll gate to the entrance of his ranch and charged twenty-five cents a team. He was flabbergasted when a man drove up one day in an automobile, for this was the first car Jordon had ever seen. "How much," asked the man, "do I owe you?" Jordon scratched his head and peered at the contraption. At last he asked: "How much horse power you got in it?" "Oh, about forty." "All right, it's two bits a span. So I figger you owe me about five dollars."

～

An Idahoan, now prominent, tells of prospecting one day in the mountains near Bonanza. He was stopped in his tracks by the sight of four beautiful pine trees, off by themselves, and enclosing a square of earth. Then he learned that, long ago, Anna King had been murdered in a dance-hall brawl. The townspeople decided that inasmuch as she had lived "differently" she should be buried "differently." In any case, she was not fit to rest with respectable persons in the cemetery. Some miners from Custer, hearing of the matter, came over and buried the girl. Today the local cemetery, containing the bones of the respectable, is a barren and desolate spot. Anna's grave is framed by four magnificent trees. It is known as the Anna King Hill cemetery, and is cared for by the Department of Forestry.

When the mayor of one of the largest Idaho cities was still a young man, he was walking past an undertaking parlor when he observed some girls carrying a casket. The mayor was asked to assist. It was explained to him that none of the ministers of the city would have anything to do with the dead person because she had been a harlot. The mayor not only assisted, but also said a few appropriate words at the funeral. On the next Sunday, his minister made some scathing remarks for the mayor's benefit, saying the woman had been too rotten to have a Christian burial, and that apparently the mayor had been the only mourner.

Strange Fauna[1]

On August 22, 1868, I wuz crossin the river at Olds Ferry when I seen somethin stickin outa the water. It pears tuh be alive, fur it don't jist drift with the current but keeps a-movin this way an that, an they's big ripples all around it. Purty soon it comes nearer an I see somethin like a elephant's trunk shootin up, an the dang thing starts tuh spoutin water—then somethin comes tuh the surface that looks like the head uv a snake, but it's ez big ez a washtub, only flat-like an hez that gol-darned horn a-stickin up out uv it an hez long, black whiskers at the sides uv its face.

By that time I wuz on the other side so I whips up my horse an rides up the side uv the hill where I cud git a good sight uv it. I gits off my horse an ties him tuh a quakin asp behind some brush an then I watches the thing. It's swimmin towards the bank. Purty soon it gits there an heaves itself outa the water an starts slitherin up the hill in my direction—an say, yuh never smelt sech a stink in all your life! My horse starts a-snortin an a-rarin, an breaks loose an lights out through the timber. An all the time that stinkin reptile is gittin closter tuh me. I make out it's about twenty feet long, an outside uv that horn that keeps shootin up an down out uv its head, an the whiskers, an a pair uv big fins, er wings, er whatever they is, all shiny-like in the sun, that comes outa the sides uv its neck, it looks down tuh the middle like a big snake, ez big around ez a calf—uv a kinda greenish-yaller color with red an black spots on it. An then all uv a suddint right then it pears tuh turn intuh a fish, with scales ez big ez yer hand, all colors uv the rainbow, shinin like big

---

1 As told by an old-timer in Swan Valley.

pieces uv colored glass in the sun—an then all the shinin
peters out an all the rest uv it is jist a grayish colored horny
tail, like a big lizard's er mebbe a crocodile's—an all the way
from where that doggone horn kep shootin up an down
on its head clear down tuh the tail they's a line uv shiny
black spines with a hook on the end uv em like a porcupine's.

It keeps a-comin closter an closter to where I'm a-standin
with my rifle cocked an the closter it come, the worst it stunk.
I'm feelin purty sick but I sez tuh myself no sech critter ez
that oughta be let tuh live. An I gits a draw on it an lets it
have a slug in the eye. It gives a beller an raises up on its
tail twenty feet high an starts fer me a-hissin an a-snarlin.
Its mouth is open a foot wide showin fangs ten inches long
an a red forked tongue that keeps a-dartin in an out a-spurtin
green pizen. I lets it have another slug in its yaller belly—
an it drops an thrashes around on the ground a-hissin an
a-snarlin an a-bellerin somethin awful, tearin up the earth,
an knockin down brush an trees, an smashin everythin
around it.

Bye an bye it's still, an I goes tuh take a look. It's a-layin
on its back an I see it's got twelve short legs a-growin out uv
its belly; the first pair, next tuh the tail, hez hoofs on em,
the next pair hez long claws ez sharp ez razors, an the next
hoofs agin, then two pairs uv claws, an the last below the
fins, er wings, er whatever they is, is hoofs agin. An everywhere I see, they's black patches where it's spit pizen, an
everythin it's teched is a-witherin an a-dyin—trees an bushes
an grass an everythin.

Well, I goes tuh git me some kind uv a rig tuh take the
critter tuh town in. I calculate tuh have it stuffed an show
it at the fair fer so much a head, an mebbe make a little
money off'n it. I gits a team an a dead-ax wagon an six
fellers tuh help me haul it down tuh the wagon an load it, fer
we can't drive right up tuh where it is on accounta the timber. I tell em tuh wear gloves an I takes a old tarp along
tuh wrap around the speciment so's when we handle it we
won't none uv us git pizened.

When we're a hundred rods er so from the place, we be-
gins tuh smell that stink agin an the horses ack skeered. I'm
a-drivin an I try tuh quiet em down but they keep on
a-snortin an a-rarin an two uv the other fellers has tuh git
out an hold em down but we can't do nothing with em so I
got tuh back a ways till I find a place tuh turn an then I

turns round an heads em the other way. We leave one feller there with the team an the rest uv us goes on.

It tain't no pleasant trip fer the nearer we git the worst the atmosphere gits. I don't know how I looked but the other fellers hez aholda their noses an wuz lookin purty pale around the gills. One feller got sick an didn't come no further.

When we gits there we see where the ground is all tore up, an the brush all trampled down fer fifty foot, an quakin asps an cottonwoods knocked down an a-layin on the ground —an everthin the pizen hit wuz dead. But nary sight uv the critter. But we finds its trail along the flattened grass an busted brush, an it leads down an smack intuh the river.

We waited round fer the rest uv the day an half the town wuz there with us watchin the river, fer they'd heard about the strange critter; but nobody sees hide ner hair uv it, ner spout ner tail.

They say a snake don't die till sundown. I dunno what the durn thing wuz, but mebbe it went down in the water tuh die—or mebbe it *didn't* die.

Boy an man, I've hunted an trapped an fished all over the state fer nigh ontuh seventy-five year, I've ketched some purty queer fish by hook an trap, but I ain't never seen nothin tuh compare with that speciment.

A Few Early Newspaper Items

Idaho World, April 18, 1872: There is a fellow in Silver City who makes a "stand off" between God and the devil by attending Sunday School on Sunday forenoon and running a faro game in the afternoon.

The district court granted Mrs. Frances Sage a divorce on last Sunday evening and took a recess for a week.

Boise News, Jan. 9, 1864: The McGinley family will give one of their chaste entertainments at the Magic Temple this evening and another one tomorrow, Sunday evening.

Boise News, Oct. 15, 1864: Justice Walker's Court— Oct. 13th. Joseph Enochs fined costs of arrest and trial for breaking and disarranging cigars in Kramer's store. William Jennison fined $20 for hitting John Griffiths a slap in the face, was satisfied with the verdict and inquired what it would cost to whip him all he wanted to.

Idaho Statesman, Sept. 15, 1864: Some fellow enamored of a young lady named Anna Bread dropped the following from his pocket:

> While belles their lovely graces spread
> And fops around them flutter,
> I'll be content with Anna *Bread*
> And won't have any *but her.*

Idaho World, April 18, 1872: LOST ONE.—Mrs. Victoria Woodhull has lost one of her husbands. Dr. Woodhull died a few days ago from intemperance assisted by an overdose of morphine.

An advertisement:

MARCH TO THE MUSIC!

Ye Hawk-Eyes, Suckers, Pukes, Wolverines, and the Public Generally Are invited to call at the Auction and Commission Store where you will find the best assortment of Fancy and Staple Groceries, Wines, Liquors, Provisions and Miners' Tools at the

Most Reasonable Prices

for the Dust which is much needed by the subscriber at the

HAWK-EYE STORE

No. 313 Wall Street   Nov. 3, 1863   Bannack City

Boise News, Jan. 23, 1864: Proceedings in Justice's Court. One of the richest little trials of the season took place in Justice Walker's court on Sunday morning. Henry Myers, who looked as if he had laid under the snow all winter instead of being the petted husband of an affectionate wife whose caresses and embraces, to say nothing of chastisements, he has enjoyed for the past seven years, was arraigned on complaint of his better half, charged with assault and battery which the complaining witness insisted on coupling with a prospective application for divorce.

Geo. C. Hough, District Attorney, and R. B. Snelling, appeared for the Territory and Frank Miller for the defense.

Defendant's counsel apologized for the uncouth appearance of his client, explaining that he had lain all night in jail and had not been given time to make his toilet.

From the testimony it was evident that the husband had struck the first blow but it was equally evident—or indications lie—that the wife had got the best of the fight.

John Fortman, who acted as peacemaker and whose conception of an oath seemed to be that a witness was required not only to *swear* but to *curse,* swore roundly and profanely to the circumstances of the fight, repeating his oath at the end of each sentence.

He had held the defendant down while the wife pulled off one of the defendant's boots with which she beat his face to a jelly. On being questioned why he permitted this, he swore, and roundly swore, that his finger was between the defendant's teeth and that he had no alternative, not wanting to part with his finger, than to leave it there and stay with it; so he let her pound away.

The justice remarked, as this was a kind of family broil in which the defendant had got the worse of it, he would be easy on him, and only fined him $10 and costs.

Boise News, Feb. 6, 1864: On Christmas Eve, the beautiful princess, daughter of the celebrated chief of the Nez Perces, Lawyer, was led to the hymeneal altar, clothed in blushes of modesty and superbly worked leggings all covered with precious gems or other kinds of beads. The happy bridegroom is a nephew of a sub-chief of the royal nation. Many a white man felt a chill at the heart at seeing this beautiful and royal damsel led to the altar to become the loved bride of one of the bravest of brave.

We cannot give an accurate description of the splendid dress worn on the occasion by the princess. Suffice it to say that the leggings were of brilliant hue; her shawl of matchless design and value; and more—*she wore no hoops*—but allowed her own development of form to fill the outlines where others less perfect have to depend on hoops and cotton. Her petticoats and tunic set very gracefully, and over her shoulders waved the beautiful locks of hair which graced her head.

Of the groom, we can only say he was dressed with taste, and, all in all, this was one of the most superb affairs ever seen, and as they retired to their soft couch of costly furs, we had to leave, and consequently can only say they each had an armful of joy.

(Immediately following in the same column) : Ye pining, lolling, screwed-up, wasp-waisted, putty-faced, consumption-mortgaged and novel-devouring daughters of fashion and idleness, you are no more fit for matrimony than a pullet is to look after a family of fifteen chickens.

*Tall
and Broad*

A Matter of Finance

Shoshone Falls, with a drop of 212 feet, had a mighty interesting formation. Long ago, when the West was being settled, a Jew and a Scotchman heard that a nickel had been lost on the Oregon Trail, and after weeks of scouting and sleuthing, they became convinced that the lost fortune was somewhere along Snake River in central Idaho. By agreement they started digging for the coin, working toward one another, one going west and the other east. Shoshone Falls marks the place of their meeting: the Scotchman was 212 feet deeper than the Jew.

A Good Drink Spoiled

The Indians of the Coeur d'Alene and Nez Perce tribes differ considerably in their intelligence and in their response to modern conveniences. One day a chief of one tribe was to meet and discuss some weighty matters with a chief of the other tribe. They took a suite on the top floor of a Lewiston hotel; and when, after several days, no one remembered having seen either chief come or go, a bellhop went up to investigate. In the middle of the floor he found a tepee, and in its doorway sat the chief of the Coeur d'Alenes, arms folded, a look of virtuous serenity on his face. "Where's your pal?" asked the bellhop. The only answer was a scornful, "Wah-huh." Again and again the question was asked but the answer was always, "Wah-huh." Going into the bathroom, the bellhop found the chief of the Nez Perces, sitting in the tub with a tomahawk in his skull. Upon demanding why he had done such a thing, the Coeur d'Alene grunted scornfully. "Big Chief, he spoilum good spring water!"

Watch Your Diet

One farmer reports that starving Chinese pheasants are in every winter a drain on his granaries and feels that the State Game Department ought to do something about it.

Last winter, after feeding all his wheat and barley, he got the idea of mixing sawdust in the rations, and was gratified to observe that the birds found it palatable. By the time spring came he was feeding chiefly sawdust; but it is reported now that in the Jerome area several pheasants are running around with broods of woodpeckers.

Plain Bad Luck

Russ Bryant tells many a whopping tale of misfortune. When listening to the hard-luck stories of others, he pulls one out of the bag and the complainers return abashed to silence. There is the time, for instance, when, with eight other men, he was shooting the White Horse Rapids: "Bad luck? Why, great guns and little pistols! We went down there in a boat, with the water pouring in white madness like frightened avalanches of snow, and with the boat disappearing for hours at a time. We were lost in a fog of cold steam, in the thunderous roar of cascades; and it isn't any wonder at all that all eight of those guys got drowned. One by one they disappeared and I never saw them again. That was tough luck enough, but it wasn't the worst of it by a mile. I was lost in the churning torrent and swam round and round in a white wilderness of geysers and rain. And, believe it or not, when I got out, I found I was on the wrong side of the river!"

Thanks Just the Same

Down in Malad Valley, Big Andy had been drinking; and when time came to go home to his wife, he decided to ride with a man named Jones because Jones had a load of hay. But while journeying, most of the load slid off, with Andy atop it, still pulling lustily from his bottle. He must have sat there an hour, drinking and smiling benignly, before another man came along. "Hello," he said, "you want a ride?" "No, thanks," said Andy, waving his bottle, "I'm riding with this guy."

Hard Times

"You fellers don't know what hard times are," said an old prospector. "Why, I remember when we fattened turkeys on gold nuggets. You could buy a turkey for four dollars and sell the gizzard for fifteen."

The Devoted
Rattler

They Make Excellent Pets[1]

When I was just a wee lad I wanted to be a cowboy and it was then that I found out what a swell friend a rattlesnake could be. I was riding through a pass one day when I saw a rattler pinned under a stone: dismounting, I made ready to kill him, but changed my mind. Didn't seem fair. So I pushed the rock off and went home. As I went along I kept hearing funny noises behind me and looked back and saw it was that silly snake. It came right to my cabin and I opened some canned milk; and that snake drank it all, and you could just see the gratitude in his eyes. He stayed around and got so friendly he slept under my bed.

One night I was sleeping soundly when a bang awakened me. I could hear someone panting and struggling, so I grabbed my gun and said, "Hands up! If you move it wouldn't surprise me if I shot something!" A loud voice yelled, "For God's sake, take this damned thing off of me!" I lit a candle. There, sprawled on the floor, was a guy who had sneaked in to steal my gold dust. But my rattler had wrapped himself around the man's leg and the leg of the table—and had his tail through the keyhole, rattling for the sheriff!

A Long High Jump

An old-timer in Lewiston was the first Idahoan to go up in a balloon. According to him, the sponsors of the flight could find nobody who would tackle the bag; and after looking it over, the old-timer said he'd go. "All the folks was lily-livered, but I says if a man could ride herd on some of the toughest broncs in Idaho, he hadn't orter be afraid of a contraption like that. So I says, 'I'll go up in the durned thing,' and I did. They had it tied down, but it warn't long before it give a fair to middlun buck and broke the hobble. And there I was, sailun round and round in the sky all by myself. 'Twarn't so bad at first, but after it got dark and I was still a-sailun I got kinda mad. By gum, I had enough and overboard I jumped. The worst thing is that I sunk clean to my knees in the pavement of Portland."

---

1 By Mrs. Jennie E. Schmelzel, Coeur d'Alene.

A Family Pet

Acme Sulphide came in from his prospect on Caribou Creek, bringing a big cougar to Larry Frazee's taxidermist shop. "Want him skun out and made into a rug?" asked Larry.

"No sir. Stuff him as is. I wouldn't think of walkun on Petronius."

"Why not? Just a cougar, ain't he?"

"Not by your tin horn. He's an institution, that's what he is. When he was just a kitten I ketched him by the mine shaft. Him and Pluto, they was great friends until Petronius growed up. Then one evening when I comes back, why Pluto was gone and Petronius wouldn't eat his supper. I was plumb mad, but I figgered Pluto was gettun old and wasn't so much account nohow. Then, by gum, I missed Mary, the goat. When I missed the last of the chickens and Petronius showed up with feathers in his whiskers, I made up my mind to shoot him. But I got to thinkun how that goat could butt, and the hens wasn't layun anyhow. So I let it go. But I shoulda bumped him then.

"Lydie, she's my old woman—or she was. Partner of my joys and sorrows for forty years. One evening when I gets back she was gone. No sign of her anywhere exceptun one shoe. And Petronius didn't want no supper agin. That got me mad, danged if it didn't, and I went for my gun to blast the varmint. Then I got to thinkun. Lydie wasn't much for looks and besides, she was about to leave me. She was all for hittun the trail, so I puts my gun up."

"Then what happened?"

"Well, last night he jumped me on the trail and took a big hunk right out of me. That was too danged much. So mount him up pretty. He repersents my whole family."

A Bouquet for Britain

One of the old-timers who became a legendary figure was Catcreek Bob. Of the countless stories associated with his name is this one. An Englishman came over to visit him, and Bob and the Englishman went hunting. They found a skunk. It ran into a hollow tree and Bob sent Axel, the hired man, after it; but unable to endure the stench, Axel came out making hideous faces. Bob then went in

*A Family
Pet*

and returned, making worse faces than Axel's. "You go in,"
Bob said to the Englishman, expecting to see the man come
out, blaspheming terribly. He was too astounded to speak
when the skunk came out and winked and made a face of
disgust and walked away.

Hail and Farewell

"Hail?" said an old-timer scornfully after listening to a
dozen stories. "Why, it don't hail no more. It usta, by the
chumblechooks! I remember one time I was out in my old
whitetop when I see a wall of hail comun that reached plumb
from the sky to the earth. I whacked them-there old plow
nags on their shin bones and we headed for home. We went
like old sixty, with that storm right at the rear wheels; and
when I got home and dashed into the machine shed, I
couldn't get my breath for nigh half a hour. Then I looked
around me and was I rum-guzzled to see that the rear end
of the old buggy was loaded with hail as big as hen's eggs.
All the way home I had kept just half a buggy length ahead
of the storm."

The Poor Provider

Nearly a century ago, a rough and dirty and bearded
miner was standing in the doorway of a saloon when to
his utter astonishment he saw a friend staggering down the
street under a cargo of flour. For a moment the man in the
doorway watched and squirted his juice and rumbled with
amazement. Then, turning to another man, he said with
infinite disgust: "Look at that-there crazy son-of-a——
a-packun home a half a ton of flour. I bet he ain't got a
pint of whisky in the house!"

A Slow Train

Some trains in northern Idaho are as slow as the one
out of Salmon City. Between Lewiston and Kamiah it's so
slow that farmers who load hay at Kamiah discover that
the cars are empty by the time they reach Lewiston, because
cows along the way have eaten it. One time a salesman
was so indignant that he swore to high heaven he could get

A Slow Train

out and walk and arrive more quickly. The conductor gazed
at him for a moment and sighed. "So could I," he said, "but
the company won't let me."

Heavy Weather[1]

My grandfather in early days rose one morning to find
that a stiff wind had blown all his chickens against the barn
and held them there. Having heard that in Idaho Falls there
was a contraption for measuring the velocity of a wind, he
set forth, and discovered that it was a fifty-foot pole set
in the earth, with a log chain fastened to the top. When the
wind blew the chain out parallel with the earth, it was a
pleasant breeze all right; but when it began popping links
off the end, it was a fair gale. When the chain let loose
altogether and traveled like a kite, then it was a wind that
meant business. That's the kind that had his roosters pinned
to the barn.

The Good Old Days

A hungry forest ranger, far from his camp, had only
one shell in his gun. Seeing a plump quail, he decided to try
for it and aimed and fired. He killed the quail all right.
When he walked over to pick it up, he learned that an elk,
not far away, had fallen in a lake from the sudden shock
and was drowning; and as he waded out to drag it to shore,
his boots filled with water, and upon emptying them he
found he had a dozen fish.

1 From the daughter of an old-timer.

The Man Who Came Apart

In 1883 Sam Gordon swore there was gold in them-there hills, and in spite of warnings that Indians would get him, he loaded his burro and set out. When he arrived at Prairie Flats he suddenly found himself surrounded by red warriors and he knew he would have to think fast. First, with a mighty gesture, he grabbed his old straw hat off his head and hurled it to the ground and jumped on it. Next, he yanked his wig off and revealed to the astonished warriors a pate as round and barren as a full moon. Losing no time, he then opened his mouth wide and yanked out both plates of false teeth and held them up to the flabbergasted stare of the red men, who by this time were almost paralyzed with fright. With one wild whoop they turned and fled; and it has been declared that the dust of their retreat was visible as far away as Boise.

Cougar Tamers

Yup, we usta have quite a bit of trouble with cougars and we wuz pretty keerful to have a gun with us when we ambled out. One time though, I plumb forgot my gun and I had a narrow squeak with one of them-there varmints. 'Twas over to that place I usta have in the valley. I goes out after supper to bring the cows home and I was right dog-eared busy when I happened to look up. There was a cougar comun down the hill after me, and me without a gun. I had to think right smart about it. When the varmint got up to me with wide open mouth I just reached in and grabbed his tail and turned him wrong side out quickern a flash. Of course, he was headed in the wrong direction then, and so doggone surprised that he went lickety-split right back up the hill and out of sight.

You Couldn't Fool Pewee

Pewee was a mighty smart dog up in northern Idaho. When his master went out fishing or hunting, Pewee was right there, chasing birds up trees or bears into gopher holes. One day the master thought to deceive him and slipped a fishing rod into his gun case; but when he went out to the yard, there was Pewee, industriously digging for worms.

The Man Who
Came Apart

Pigs Is Pigs

Proud of his own bronco-busting powers, Walt wanted his son to emulate him, and chose for him one day the scurviest pinto he could find. The lad was thrown higher than a kite and came down with the sound of an earthquake; and the old man was right upon him, whanging with both hands. "What's the matter, boy? When I was your age I rid the wust broomtail plumb to the blasted blue blazes, and here you be throwed highern the 1929 stock market!" The lad argued piteously that a pig had scared his pony; whereupon the old man roared: "You git down the lane there. I'll ride him and as I come boltun past hickey-split, you jump out like a pig and see if I'm throwed!" The lad went down the lane; and when he heard his father coming he sprang out and squealed, and the pony doubled into a sunfish that sent the old fellow higher than the poplar trees. Gathering himself, he turned purple with rage. "You half-witted doodle-bug! I said to jump out like a pig, not like a gad-danged hog!"

Money by the Gallon

The Norwegians northwest of Moscow are thrifty folk. Hans and his wife Helen, for instance, have not only their homestead, but also three other farms which they have purchased. Formerly they kept their savings in cream cans; and one day, when time drew near for payment on the third farm, Helen fetched a can and began to pour the savings out. She counted the money until she had eight thousand dollars; whereupon, knowing that the can was supposed to contain ten thousand, she screamed. "Hans," she yelled, "we've been robbed! There's only eight thousand dollars!" Hans came over and looked at her and then at the can. "Helen, you fool," he said, "I'm about to lose my patience with you. Can't you ever see! You've got the wrong can!"

A Big Snow

There have been deep winters in Idaho. In one, many years ago, some shepherds pitched camp for the night after rounding their sheep into a group, and awoke the next morning to discover that it had snowed foot upon foot.

To their consternation the sheep were gone. "But look," said one, pointing to a thousand small mounds over the landscape. And so it was: the sheep had all been snowed under and now seemed to be about the size of pillows under the snow.

A Bear for Work

Paul Peavy was in town from his logging camp buying supplies when Ted Chelde asked: "What in darnation you feedun so much honey to lumberjacks for? Ain't that pretty fancy feed for them?"

"This honey ain't for them. It's an investment."

"How come?" propounded Ted.

"Well, I make lumberjacks leave their coats in camp and in freezun weather I get more out of them. But it ain't enough. So I got the idea to make my silvertip cub work too. He's crazy about honey and will climb a rainbow to get it. So I strap a pair of broadaxes on his feet, and give him a sniff at a can and then shin up a tree with it. Up comes Annabel, the axes scoring the tree on two sides. Then I lower the can and down he goes, and raise it and up he shins, just hewing the tree as smooth as a whistle. Then to make railroad ties all I gotta do is chop it over and whack it up into lengths."

Gold Strike in Hell.

A Bear
for Work

Gold Strike in Hell

An old prospector who never ran in luck died and went to heaven, but the place was so crowded he could not get in. St. Peter told him to hang around awhile and there might be room. After pondering the matter, the old fellow called an angel and whispered to him that there had been a gold strike down in hell; and at once there was a pell-mell rush of angels, and soon heaven was empty. As the horde fled downward, the prospector gazed after it hungrily and then turned to Peter. "You know," he said, "mebbe there was some truth in that rumor."

Big As an Idaho Potato

Yes, I'n tell you about wolves. My partner and me, we went up in the Sawtooths and got two elk and was headun home when we looked around and seen eleven wolves after us. We cut a elk loose and they et that. In another mile we give them the other elk and they et that. Then we left our horses and run for it, and they came up and et the horses. I said to my partner that I would rest and shoot a wolf and then run while he was restun and then he could shoot one. So we did. I shot one and the wolves pounced on it while I was runnun; and then my partner, he shot one. Well, we kept that up till we had shot ten of them. Then my partner yelled, "God a-mighty, Jim, look!" I looked behind me and there right on our tails was the biggest wolf anybody ever laid eyes on. He was as big as a house. And then I remembered he'd have to be that big, seeing as how he'd et two elk, two horses, and ten wolves.

No Bounty for Varmints

Gunnysack Johnson came in from his house on Flat Creek, acting mysteriously. "You the sheriff?" he asked.

"Sure," said Bib Holstead. "What's on your mind?"

"I got suthin on it, all right. I been worried right smart about it and I can't stand it no longer, so here I be. I been homesteadun on Flat Creek since the winter of the big snow."

"Hain't you got pretty lonesome there?"

" 'Twarn't bad as it mighta been. When I went in I had

a dollar watch and the tick season was on. When I wasn't windun the watch I was a-scratchun tick bites. I was gettun kinda hungry for someone to talk to when in blows a sociable cuss and we gets to gabbun and he wants to know why I'm off by myself. I told him I'd been cleaned by a stock sales-man and run off where I wouldn't never see one again. 'That's strange,' says he. 'I'm a stock salesman myself and I can let you in on the ground floor on a block of First Col-lateral Trust Indentures Consolidated.' "

"Go on," said Bib. "What happened?"

"I bumped him off. I couldn't stand it. An then I decided I was headed to come clean, so here I be. What do I get?"

"Not a durned cent. We quit payun bounty on them guys ten years ago."

A Problem in Economics

One morning I was sitting on the front porch when I looked up to see a fellow staggering with both arms full of groceries, a gallon jug of sirup on his head. He stumbled, and the jug struck a stone and the sirup spilled. Saying he did not want to lose all the sirup, the man asked my mother to do him a pile of pancakes in a hurry; and this she did, and the hungry fellow set to with a will. Three of us carried pancakes to him, all of which he ate with great gusto; where-upon, after licking his lips a time or two and gazing ex-pectantly around him, he swallowed the rock.

Riding Rainbows

Squint Hocum landed his skiff at the fish hatchery one day last week. "Hi, Joe," he yelped, "I want a few pinters about handlun fish."

"Fish? I thought you was running a stock ranch."

"Was a stock ranch, but this high water raised the lake and turned her into a fish ranch. One hundred and sixty acres all fenced and cross fenced with hog wire."

"And you're stocking her with fish?"

"The high water tended to that—leastways give me a start. But it wasn't long till them durned fish found a gate open and went back into the lake."

"Tough luck. What did you do?"

"Durn near ruined me, that's what it done. Them fish

Riding
Rainbows

went out to graze every morning, and I had a heck of a time gettun them back into my corral. Fact is, I never would of done it without Elmer."

"Who's Elmer?"

"One of them rainbow trout you planted in the lake year ago. He growed so big I roped him and broke him to ride. Oh, he was skittish at first—tender on the bit and sunfished right smart if I roweled him. Dang near drownded me a time or two when he dove. But when he got contrary I'd dangle a bunch of angleworms at the end of a fishline and ride him plumb straight. Got him gentled down, I did. Now I don't never need a bridle."

"Don't, eh? Where's Elmer now?"

"Got a saddle gall. Now as I was sayun, you know fish and I don't, so just give me some pinters about the critters."

Joe shook his head and gurgled. "About fish? You askun me!"

When Manhood Was in Power

In early times, it was difficult to get teachers in mining towns, or at least it was difficult to persuade them to remain. Any male pupil, from five years up, would yank out a revolver and threaten to blow the teacher's brains out if that unfortunate and intimidated gentleman said anything the youngster did not like. Not only that: some of these boys could curse a blue streak, and often did so right in the middle of a school lesson.

Because teachers came and vanished so often, the school boards ruled that the pupils had to be searched for concealed pistols, knives, and tobacco each morning before entering the schoolroom. The first two items were not hard to expose, and in consequence teachers were more willing to stay after they had been brought in from Eastern states. Tobacco was another matter. The youngsters could still sneak in with their small plugs and use a little bag of sawdust as a spittoon. It was not unusual for them to chew tobacco and slyly spit the juice into the sawdust; but the time passed when they were allowed to march into the schoolhouse with a dagger and a pistol at their waists.

In those days, too, there was no law to prevent schoolboys from buying drinks over the counter at the nearest saloon, and this was a frequent sight.

Snakes

There are dozens of rattlesnake stories told in Idaho. These are the reports of a sheepherder as told to Maurice L. Russell. The man was out in the foothills one night, stone sober, and at dusk pitched his camp; but suspecting that there were snakes in the area, he found two short pieces of rope and swung a hammock between two trees. In the morning he was awakened by a strange jerking at his bed. Upon sitting up and peering, he saw that instead of ropes he had used two rattlers, both of which had been dormant because of the cold. This sheepherder also tells this one: "I pitched my bed one night by a little creek. Hours later I felt something wigglun in bed and so I hops out and sets by the fire the rest of the night. And, by gad, the next mornun that old mattress was so plumb swole up that I used it for a feather bed for two weeks."

Just Home Folks

In the late forenoon of a hot August day, a lone traveler drove his team and wagon into the yard of a wayside hotel. The furniture was of boards, boxes, and kegs. On the dining table were old bottles, most of them empty, and all of them dirty; cups and plates of the coarsest ware; glasses as thick as the man's thumb. The spout of the cream pitcher was gone, the sugar bowl was cracked, and the molasses jar was black with flies. Instructed to stable his beasts, the man went to the barn but in a moment was back in the hotel, hot and indignant. "I can't put my horses in that stable," he said. "Why, there's millions of flies in that stable!" The landlady wiped her nose on a big red arm and looked back over her shoulder at the kitchen clock. "Well, jist wait about twenty minutes," she said wearily, "and they'll all be in the dining room."

Without a Diploma

Horns Wolf snowshoed into Cedar Flat the other day, where old Yubie Dan was holed up for the winter. "Murder in a roadhouse!" snorted Horns. "Smells powerful ratty in this cabin."

"Guess you mean Hal," said Yubie, proud-like.

"Who's Hal?"

"Why, darn your tootun, he's my eddicated packrat."

"I knowed you was plumb worthless when the telegraph company kicked you out but I never thought you'd shack up with a rat, the smelly varmint. It ain't only the odor, as you might say, usun your eddicated language. It's the way they bang the roof."

"You offend me," said Yubie. "Hal is eddicated, like I said. A packrat will carry off anything but he allus replaces it with something else. So I throw my tin cans in the woodbox, leavun wood piled outside; and Hal, he takes the cans out and brings the wood back. It saves a heap of labor."

"But how about bangun the roof all night?"

"Oh, that. Why, I learnt him the Morse code so now he shins up the roof, takes a squint at the sun or the moon, and taps out the time with his tail. That saves me trouble, too. But as I says, he's an eddicated rat."

Racehorse Eggs

Because of its fertility, many Easterners were attracted in former times to Paradise Valley in northern Idaho. An old-timer liked to show to visitors the enormous pumpkins which were grown there; and when asked what they were, he answered, "Why, them's hoss eggs. Never seen any afore?" A little later he would stagger around with an unusually huge pumpkin and pretend to stumble and drop it; whereupon it would roll down a hill and start up a rabbit from a colony at the foot of the hill; for the pumpkin would hit a stone and explode with an awful bang. One Easterner, seeing a rabbit bounding off at full speed, cried excitedly: "Well, by gum, that egg would certainly have made some racehorse!"

Steak on the Hoof

I aimed at the grizzly's breast and pulled the trigger. Stunned for a moment, he rose to his hind feet and made a fearful face. Then he went down, licked at the blood spurting from him, and considered me. He was so close now I could see the green in his eyes and feel the hunger in his breath. I tried agin, but my gun jammed. Escape was impossible. I was doomed. And then, as the beast drew near,

I went mad: I screamed and made hideous sounds, knowing that I would be eaten; and thereupon fell (or thought I did) in a black swoon. .... When I opened my eyes I was astounded to find blood and fur on my hands; and upon turning over, to perceive how enormous my belly was. It was an hour before the horrible truth dawned on me: in my wild delirium I had eaten the bear!

Lost Lake

There usta be fine hosses in this-here north Idaho country. Boosephalis was raised right here and usta range in Lawyer's Canyon. Sheridan's black hoss was a colt on the Camas Prairie, and Lady Godiva got her white hoss from a herd over near Kamiah. But the famousest hoss that ever roamed this range was the Strawberry Roan. He used to water in a little lake over near Craig Mountain; but one night thousands of ducks lit on that lake and it froze over; and when the old roan come there to drink and saw them, he snorted like the blue blazes of wrath; and the terrified ducks, unable to get their feet loose, flew away with the lake.

A White Elephant

Into an early mining town in Idaho one morning, there came a pack train of eleven mules, ten of them loaded with whisky and one with flour. A group of miners left a saloon and sauntered out to inspect the freight; and upon seeing what the cargo was on most of the mules, they were pleased. At last, however, one came to the cargo on the eleventh mule and fell back, appalled. He turned to his companions. "What in the name of hell," he asked, "are we going to do with all that flour?"

Slow Train

Among intolerably slow trains in Idaho is the branch to the Twin Falls area. Once an impatient passenger wanted to know of the conductor why the train had stopped. "There's a cow on the track," he said. "We have to chase her off." When, a little later, the train stopped again, the passenger roared: "Now what's wrong?" "Oh," said the conductor serenely, "we just caught up with the cow."

Lost
Lake

Mud in Moscow

Before Moscow was paved, the autumn rains turned the streets into such depth of mud that it was unsafe to journey after nightfall. Many a freighting team got bogged and had to be left until spring, though they were fed by ferrying hay and water to them down a cable. After several seasons of disaster, pontoon bridges were built; and one day a fuzzy old man from Texas, carrying too much bad whisky, slipped off a bridge and sank in to his waist. A cowboy roped him and he was dragged out, though his boots, which were his pride, his investment, were left behind. He was so furious that he threatened to sue the town; and the next spring extensive excavations were made, but the boots were never recovered. The indignant old fellow walked all the way back to Texas barefooted.

The Waltz Triumphant

A prospector came down from the mountains in the Yankee Fork area, and on his way passed through a very narrow canyon. In it he met a bear, a huge brown bear with anger in his eyes. There was not room for the man and the bear to pass, so the man, having no gun, fell to his hands and knees and began to prance absurdly, and was gratified after a few minutes to find the beast imitating him. After the two waltzed around a bit, the man minced up to the bear and kissed him on one cheek; and after a bit of reflection the bear did likewise. Then they went through a French four, a reel, and several measures of a quadrille. By this time the beast was so flabbergasted and so confused in his directions that he waltzed back down the canyon the way he had come and the prospector followed.

Muskeeters

Idaho is not for the most part a mosquito state, but many stories are told of the pests. In a Boise beer parlor a group of men were talking. Said one: "Why, dang it, up in McCall the muskeeters is so gad-plumb thick that if you wanta talk to a person you have to throw a brick at him and then talk through the hole." "Yeh?" said another man.

"Well, down in Twin Falls, all you gotta do is whirl a pint cup around your head and you ketch a quart of muskeeters any time."

Just Set

In the old days, we didn't have no automobiles and paved roads and all sich fancy likes. We didn't even have no trails and bridges. One time I 'member my wife was sick and I had to go to Orofino for to bring a doctor. But when I got to the river I couldn't figger out how to cross. I decided to jump but when I was about three-fourths across I seen I wouldn't make it so I come back to think some more. Then I had to put my mind to it. There was a big tree on the edge of the river, so I hooked my lasso on a limb and got back and run for it, using the lasso to give me a swing across. That was good thinkun, but not everybody woulda 'membered the lasso would bring him right back agin if he wasn't durned keerful. Me, I cut the lasso when I was half way across. I tell you, I don't know what some of them-there modern squirts woulda done in a case like that. Just set on the bank, I guess.

Ordeal by Water

Formerly, but not today, the summers in Lewiston baked everything to a cinder, including the hills. Water in the Snake and Clearwater Rivers often boiled at the edges, though not in midstream where the current was faster. Many an old-timer had his beard catch fire; and to take care of this matter, barrels of water were set up and down the sidewalks. One day a newcomer appeared suddenly in midafternoon, and the sun, shining on his red beard, gave it the appearance of flame. The whole town rushed to his aid with pails of water and drenched him; but because his acreage of whiskers kept shining undiminished, they next doused him with whole barrels and discovered after it was too late that they had drowned him. This is said to have been the only charitable murder ever committed in the town.

Frontier Burial

When northern Idahoans complain of the cold winters, old-timers snort with disgust and declare how cold it used to be in former times. It was not so much that they were

unable to blow out the frozen flames of their lamps. It was
chiefly their difficulty in burying their dead because of
deeply frozen ground. After awhile they solved their problem by laying the dead persons outside and letting them
freeze as hard as spikes; whereupon they put pointed iron
shoes on their feet and stood the corpses upright and drove
them like piles into the earth.

The Fence That Moved

As told by a cowboy: I was punchun cows near Lewiston.
The boss said Swede and me, we was to cut posts for a long
fence and so we got our tools and set out. Swede said he
smelt something danged rotten but I said it smelt like dead
snakes but he said it was too cold for snakes to be out. Just
the same, we went up a hill and there was thousands of
rattlesnakes that had crawled out and got froze as stiff as a
wagon tire. "By golly," I said, "why not use them for fence
posts?" And so we did. He'd stick the small end down and
I'd set on my horse and pound on the head with a twenty-
pound hammer and drive the snake into the frozen ground.
Well, we set two miles of them-there posts and felt mighty
proud. When we told the boss what we'd done, he said,
"Let's go out and see," and so we went out. And, by gad, you
know what? The sun had come out and thawed them varmints, and there they was, wiggling to beat all get-out and
tanglun that barbwire up till it was plumb ruined.

A Bear-Faced Lie

From the logging camps north of Payette it was the
custom of the men to go to town now and then for a good
drink. On his return journey, one of the men met a huge
grizzly bear and shinned up a tall slender tree; and after
pondering a moment the bear went after him. The tree
began to bend and the farther the man climbed the more it
bent, until he knew he would have to use his wits. With his
pocketknife he cut the top of the tree off and sharpened it,
and then let go and fell to the earth. The sudden release of
the tree hurled the bear ten feet into the sky; and when the
beast came down, he was speared by the sharpened tree that
went through him and held him fast.

The Fence
That Moved

New Jersey Terror

A group of men were talking in a Shoshone pool hall about mosquitoes. A little runt of a cowpuncher listened for an hour before he said, "You guys, you ain't seen nothun. Why, down around Rupert there's real mosquiters. Once, when I was a-wranglun the critters, I pitched my buffalo robe and staked my hoss; when along comes two mosquiters as big as caribou. They looks me over and one says, 'I don't think he'd make us a meal. He might do for dessert but not for the full helpuns. Let's taste his hoss.' And afore I knowed it, they had that hoss et up clear down to his galluses. Then they looks at me again. 'I tell you,' says one, 'we'll yank the shoes off the hoss and pitch hoss-shoes to see who gits him. They ain't enough in him for dessert for two.' And so they begun pitchun hoss-shoes and me a-settun there and shakun all over. Well, I'd a gone right down a mosquiter's gullet if it hadn't a been they was such ornery cusses. One accused the other of cheatun and while they was down at the stake a-figgerun out which shoe was closest, I skinned out like hell and high lightning. For ten miles I could hear them mosquiters after me. They sounded like two airplanes."

Idaho Tobacco

An old-timer, speaking of the fact that few fishermen today have any luck, declared that a lot of them use the wrong bait. Especially are those foolish who use grass-hoppers. "A grasshopper," he said, "ain't no good as bait. Why, when he sees a fish coming, he spits tobacco juice in his face. Last summer, one of the lakes up around McCall was turned brown from grasshopper tobacco juice."

A Forty-five Ninety

John Cheery was an old-timer in the Salmon River country who used to amuse his neighbors with many a whopping yarn. "When," he said, "you'n toss a flapjack up the chimbley and run out and ketch it before it hits the ground, and if it ain't got no soot on it, then, by gosh, you're a cook." A favorite with him was the time he ran out of food and went out to kill a deer. "The only gun in camp was so old I was a-scairt to tech it; but that day I grabs the old

gal aroun the barrel which looked like the stoutest part of
her and off I sets. But, by swan! When I pulled the trigger
I blowed out a rat's nest and seven young rats. Why, that
old gun wiggled and shook and squirmed so I had to drop it!"

Idaho Potatoes

In the Snake River Valley lives an old-timer who is
known as Old Jim. Old Jim comes to town now and then and
boasts of the fertility of his land, but complains that he is
unable to market the stuff. He grew pumpkins, but they
were so large he could not get them on to a wagon, and
then ventured into potatoes. When, two years ago, a CCC
camp was established near by, Old Jim was approached by
a man who wanted to buy a hundred pounds of spuds. "Only
a hundred pounds?" he asked, scratching his pate. "No, I
can't do it. I wouldn't cut a spud in two for no one."

Corpus Delicti

It was during Prohibition times that four hunters from
the East came to the ranch of John Hogan in the Coeur
d'Alene area and asked him for a pack horse. Reluctantly,
John lent them the pride of this ranch, a white mule which
he called Whitey; and soon Whitey was loaded with supplies, including two gallons of moonshine.

The first night out the mule was turned loose to pasture
and the four men gave their enthusiasm to a gallon of
whisky. They drank all of it and passed out. The mule
wandered in later, accidentally knocked the other gallon over,
spilling it, and decided that he liked the aroma; whereupon
he ate all the grass that the whisky had saturated and also
passed out, lying side by side with his masters. When the
men came to the next morning, they believed the mule was
dead, but how to convince Hogan a healthy mule had lain
down and died, they did not know. After much argument
they decided to skin the mule and return the hide as proof
that the creature was dead. This they did.

After they had gone, the mule came to, and after
shaking himself concluded that all was not as it should be.
He took one long incredulous look at his denuded self and
headed for home. Hogan was so amazed when the mule
appeared that for three hours he was paralyzed. He then

observed that Whitey was turning bluish and knew that something must be done at once. Procuring sheep pelts, he clothed the mule and fastened the pelts with thorns off blackberry bushes. Abashed, but feeling better, Whitey slunk off to the "amen" corner of the corral and took fresh stock of himself. He found his master's workmanship good and survived the winter in fine style.

He also became Hogan's most valuable piece of property; for in the next summer, John clipped seventy-four pounds of wool and picked fourteen quarts of blackberries off Whitey's hide.

Indian
Legends

The Shifting Dunes[1]

It was an autumn afternoon when Chief Tyhee, a huge man of handsome frame, visited me at my home in St. Anthony. The leader of the Bannacks and Shoshonis was still proudly erect in spite of his one hundred moons, standing six feet four in his bare feet and looking an aristocrat in every inch of him. He asked if I had noted the wonderful sunset, and we went out to have a view of it. Great shafts of amber, scarlet, and red barred the sky as the evening sun sank in its majesty of colorful draperies. Off in the northwest the huge sand dunes were dyed pink and golden.

As the colors deepened in the dunes, I called them to Tyhee's attention, but he only shrugged and gave a disdainful grunt. There was a strange look in his eyes; something unpleasant seemed to be on his mind. I asked him what about these dunes displeased him, but he said I could not

1 By W. W. Spiers, of Lava Hot Springs.

Legend of the Shifting Dunes.

understand; and again stood in aloof grandeur for a long while. When I urged him again he told me this story.

Many moons ago the Bannacks and Shoshonis were at war with the Blackfeet of Montana. There were heap big quarrels over hunting grounds; there had been heap big battles, but the largest occurred among the dunes, with thousands of warriors fighting on either side. Tyhee was only a small lad then, but he watched the fight. As the sun was sinking and the armies were engaged in a death struggle, the great dunes rose and engulfed both armies. Not a warrior escaped. The people of both tribes fled from the evil spirits infesting the dunes; and still, said Tyhee, you could hear the weird moaning and chanting of the spirits.

After Tyhee's death, his son visited me many times; and though he would not tell the story of the dunes, he declared that what his father had said was true. He pointed out also that these dunes are constantly shifting, and would someday give up their dead. No doubt in the dim past warriors did fight there, and perhaps the white and golden depths of sand enshrouded many of them. Arrowheads are still found in the shifting sands. It is interesting to speculate on the mysteries of these beautiful moving mounds that are slowly journeying year by year into the northwest.

The Thatuna Hills

Long before white men came there lived in the Panhandle of Idaho a beautiful Indian maid of the Nez Perce tribe. Her name was Thatuna. Northward lived the Coeur d'Alenes, and among them was the noble son of a chieftain. At an annual autumn festival held on the flat lands east of where Moscow now stands, these two met and loved, and the maid was carried away to her new home.

They lived happily for many years. When the old chief died, he said on his deathbed that his son was to be chief if he would return his Nez Perce wife and marry a Coeur d'Alene woman. This the young man refused to do, but his wife took their son and fled, so that her husband could become a leader. She hid herself in the hills that now bear her name, and her husband hunted everywhere for her. When discovered, she climbed to the highest point of rock on the Thatuna Hills and leapt off, rather than return and sacrifice her husband's future.

Why Doves Mourn

Long ago the dove was called Co-ah-wee-haw, an Indian representation of the bird's call. It was also named "Rattlesnake's Brother-in-law" (Toag'-go-in-dayts) because of the belief that when an Indian mocked the bird or killed its mate, it told a rattlesnake where the Indian was going and to lie in wait and bite him as he passed. If an Indian killed one of the reptiles, the dove sat in a tree and lamented with mournful cry the snake's death. It was a foolhardy Indian who mocked or killed a mourning dove.

Stories of Hayden Lake[1]

Years ago when Coeur d'Alene Indians lived near Hayden Lake, fish and wild game were scarce, the corn and wild berries froze, and there was little to eat. The medicine man advised the tribe to leave the area so that fish and game could multiply but the Indians refused to leave. In years following food became scarcer still, but the Indians would not go.

One night the chief went out in his canoe to fish. It was a moonlit night and his people saw him; and they saw him suddenly stand up and shout, declaring he had caught a fish. Then slowly the boat began to go around in circles. It gained in speed until finally it leapt into the air and plunged nose first into a whirlpool. This circumstance greatly impressed the tribe, and when again the medicine man said the Great Spirit wanted them to leave, they packed up and left. In their new home they waited year after year, but the Spirit never told them to return to Hayden Lake.

Two tribes of Indians were encamped on the shores of Hayden Lake when a warrior of one tribe fell so hopelessly in love with a maiden from the other that he abducted her and set out across the water. Dark clouds rose at once and covered the moon; a great wind became a furious hurricane. The canoe was swallowed and both were lost. For many days the wailing of squaws was heard, and for many nights council fires touched the sky. The maiden's father set out in a canoe to discover and return the lovers, but he, too, was

---

[1] Told to E. E. Beeson, of Hayden Lake, by a Coeur d'Alene Indian whose father saw the chief drowned.

drowned. From that day forth, Indians were afraid of the lake; and it is said that with the exception of a few who were hired by a moving-picture company to cross it in 1919, no Indian has ever been known to cross this water.

Spirit Lake

Beautiful Spirit Lake in northern Idaho was named for the following legend. An Indian chief's daughter was in love with an Indian brave; but her father, to keep peace with another tribe, gave his daughter to another warrior. On the night of the wedding feast, the girl and her lover slipped away and bound their wrists together and leapt into the lake. This lake, according to legend, does not give up its dead; and the nonplussed Indians declared that a spirit had carried the girl and her true love away.

Craters

There is an interesting legend concerning the Craters of the Moon. Indians say their Great White Father had set the area aside as a private and sacred hunting ground. He forbade Indians to hunt thereon, and said if they did so, the craters would become active and spread desolation over the area. One time a party of white huntsmen sought game in the region, even though terrified Indians strove to dissuade them. As a result of the desecration, the craters came alive and spouted fire and covered the area with molten lava. And such was the cause of the last eruptions.

The Water Baby

Pah-ohn-ah is not a baby nor fairy nor Nin-numbee, but it resembles a baby and lives in streams and springs, water holes and caves. A band of Indians stopped one noon near a stream. A woman took her infant baby out of the papoose board to bathe and rest it; but when the Indians resumed their journey, the infant began to fret. The mother tried to quiet it by tying a charm or sleep packet near its head. She next took a caterpillar cocoon and rubbed it across in front of the eyes and then tied it to the board. For it was the cocoon of Euh-pa, the Sleepy One. The baby still cried. Upon approaching the evening camping ground, the baby

Nin-numbee

ceased crying; and the mother, after unlacing and opening
the board, discovered that she had Pah-ohn-ah, and that it
had died for want of water. The babies had been traded at
the noon camp!

Nin-numbee

"Hush," the mother tells her children, when encamped
in certain areas, "this is where the Nin-numbees live. Do not
play near the large rocks or caves or they will take you
away."

Once a young girl was picking berries and fell in love
with a Nin-numbee and followed him away and was never
seen again. For the Nin-numbees are the spirits of departed
warriors and have an arrow case slung on their backs, and
carry a bow. They are seen or heard only late in the evenings
or very early in the mornings, and then they sing, and fortunate is the waiting warrior who learns the song. Nor must
the warrior tell of what he has seen, else it will never be
shown him again. He will lose the power imparted and will
no longer be victorious in battle.

Shoshone Cave

In the Shoshoni tribe was a handsome young buck who
was unsurpassed in running, jumping, or shooting. But
he was unhappy because he loved a princess in a neighboring
tribe with whom the Shoshonis were constantly at war.
When, in one battle, the princess was captured, the lover
sought her tent and made off with her, but in their attempt
to escape she was mortally wounded. He carried her in his
arms, looking for a burial spot and came to a cave and
entered it, finding to his surprise and delight that it was
a cave of ice. He buried her there. As the seasons passed,
the body of the princess was engulfed, and today, legend
declares, is still entombed in a wall of Shoshone Ice Cave,
north of Shoshone.

A Long Tale

Najewea was the lovely daughter of an Indian chief,
and many warriors wanted her for a wife. Not wishing to
offend anyone, the chief said she would be given to the brave
who could tell the longest story. Many competed, and long

Shoshone
Cave

were the tales the old fellow had to listen to. One story
ran for a week, and the father thought that was about as
long as any tale could be; but there came a more resourceful
buck who changed his mind. "Once upon a time there was
an ant who was ambitious. He was so ambitious he decided to move all of the Indian grain to his own storehouse
which was a hundred yards away. He carried it kernel by
kernel. It took him twenty-four hours to carry a kernel and
return." "Yes?" said the old chief impatiently. "When the
last kernel was carried, the Indians harvested and filled
their granary and the ant began carrying the crop——"
"That'll do," said the chief, seeing that this story would last
as long as Indians planted and harvested. "She's your
squaw."

Sun and Moon

In northern Idaho is the story of the Sun Sister and
Moon Brother. In a darkened house an Indian maid was
ravished at a singing party by a man whom she could not
recognize. When, later, the act was repeated, she blackened
her hands with soot and smeared his back; and then in
lamplight saw the violator was her own brother. In great
anger she cut off her breasts and gave them to him, saying,
"Since you relish me, eat these." He flew into a passion,
and she ran about the room to escape him, and then fled
into the night, taking a torch of wood to guide her. The
brother followed with another torch but he fell and almost
extinguished his light. She became the sun, and he became
the moon.

Ghosts

An Indian who can conquer a ghost can conquer a world.
In northern Idaho a young buck of exceptional strength
saw one night a terrible object that seemed to be a human
being without arms or legs. It had the appearance of a
corpse, except that it fought with unwonted vigor and re-
sourcefulness, as the Indian discovered in the uncanny contest that followed. He fought all night, and as dawn began
to come he caught a strong hold on his adversary and refused
to let him go. He continued the fight until insensible; and
upon recovering his wits learned that he was bruised and
bleeding all over but still very much alive. Wise men of the

Ghosts

tribe said if he had worsted a ghost he would be a man of superhuman strength; as indeed he proved to be, having the strength of ten giants and caring nothing for the rigors of climate.

The Legend of Swan Lake[1]

Some half-dozen miles to the east of Soda Springs, nestling in the top of a small mountain, lies a picturesque little lake known for years as Swan Lake. The name no doubt was given to it because of the peculiar shape: when viewed as a whole, it has the appearance of a swan. No doubt in ages long gone by its basin was an active volcano and supplied its portion of the many miles of lava formation to be found throughout this section of the State. Either during one of its eruptions or later, a stratum of subterranean water found its way through this fissure and formed a small lake. This water before it was taken out for irrigation purposes and mixed with other water was highly mineralized. Articles remaining at length in it would petrify, and many large branches and limbs from trees were earlier to be found on the sloping sides of the lake. In the earlier history of the State and even back to the time when only the Indian roamed these parts, there have been a number of legends connected with this picturesque body of water.

The earlier Indians carried a story that an Indian princess lost her life in the lake, the chief medicine man cursed the waters, and for years no one was able to swim across the lake. Some irresistible power pulled the swimmer down, and gravity of the person seemed treble his usual weight as soon as he entered the water. Connected with this legend was the story that there was no bottom to the lake. During my childhood I spent many hours roaming around this lake, and some endeavors were made to learn how deep it was, but I was never able to find any bottom, but we did ascertain that it was very deep and beyond the depth of any measurements at our command

At certain times in the fall of the year it was claimed that a wonderful mirage of some ancient city was to be seen in this lake. In talking with the Indians back in 1895 they gave me to understand that this mirage had been known to appear in this lake for hundreds of years back; the archi-

---

1 By W. W. Spiers.

tecture so far as I could glean from them was a semi-Gothic
nature and was a very large city. They claimed at that time
it was one of the ancient cities that earlier were found to be
on this continent and it is buried somewhere in the deserts
of Nevada. Many white people in the early history of the
State also claimed that the mirage was a fact and that the
great city had been seen by a number of people while looking
into the water.

Indian Legend of Creation.

Beliefs and
Customs

PART II—BELIEFS AND CUSTOMS

THIS section by no means pretends to be a complete coverage of its materials. The beliefs and customs included here are only those which, coming in among many others from Project workers and volunteers, seemed to be the most interesting and pertinent. It was soon discovered that most of the old-timers are rather cynically dubious of anyone who asks about their beliefs. As a matter of fact, a few of them wrote scathing letters to the office to defend their beliefs against what they took to be heretical and unwarranted snooping; while others declared that customs and beliefs of pioneers were now invested with a holiness, even if not with a scientific infallibility, that placed them beyond the scrutiny of an ungodly world.

The writer of this, born of pioneer stock himself, had formerly been aware of the resentment and suspicion; for when, several years ago, a philologist appeared to make a study of his father's speech, the old gentleman was filled with contempt and dismay. It was not realized, however, that such an attitude widely prevails among those still living who were active in conquering Idaho's frontiers. Beyond all question it does. Many old-timers, if asked about their weather signs, their beliefs, or their home remedies, will retire into their holes and have no more to do with you. Their distrust is largely defensive. The findings of science have upset their world, placed many of their beliefs under ridicule, and driven them to cherish some of their old habits with an ardor that is almost religious.

It would be necessary, therefore, to have in the field only trained and tactful persons if a real study were to be made of pioneer customs and beliefs which still survive. Every old-timer's memory is a storehouse of beliefs that the world today finds picturesque, amazing, or sometimes incredibly naïve. The weather signs and home remedies included here range, for instance, from those which beyond all doubt are trustworthy or effective to those which have been born out of utter ignorance. All of those listed are actually believed by persons still alive.

Customs

RUNYAN

❦

Pioneer Health Hints

1. It is unwise to change to cooler clothing except when you first get up in the morning.

2. Never ride with your arm or elbow outside any vehicle.

3. In stepping from any wheeled vehicle, while in motion, let it be from the rear, for then the wheels cannot run over you.

4. The man who attempts to alight from a steam car while in motion is a fool.

5. Never attempt to cross a road or street in a hurry in front of a passing vehicle for if you should stumble or slip, you will be run over. Make up the half minute lost by waiting until the vehicle has passed by increased diligence in some other direction.

6. It is miserable economy to save time by robbing yourself of necessary sleep.

7. If you find yourself inclined to wake up at a regular hour of the night and remain awake, you can break the habit in three days by getting up as soon as you wake and not going to sleep again until your usual hour of retiring; or retire two hours later and rise two hours earlier for three days in succession—not sleeping a moment in the daytime.

8. If infants and young children are inclined to be wakeful at night or very early in the morning, put them to bed later and, besides, arrange that their day nap shall be in the forenoon.

9. "Order is heaven's first law"; regularity is nature's great rule; hence, regularity in eating, sleeping, and exercise has a very large share in securing a long and healthful life.

10. If you are caught in a drenching rain or fall in the water, by all means keep in motion sufficiently vigorous to

prevent the slightest chilly sensation until you reach the house; then change your clothing with great rapidity before a blazing fire, and drink instantly a pint of some hot liquid.

11. To allow clothing to dry upon you, unless keeping up vigorous exercise until thoroughly dried, is suicidal.

12. If you are conscious of being in a passion, keep your mouth shut, for words increase it. Many a person has dropped dead in a rage.

13. If a person faints, place him on his back and let him alone; he wants arterial blood to flow to the head; and it is easier for the heart to throw it there in a horizontal line than perpendicularly.

14. If you want to get instantly rid of beastly surfeit, put your finger down your throat until free vomiting ensues, and eat nothing for ten hours.

15. Feel a noble pride in living within your means, then you will not be hustled off to a cheerless hospital in your last sickness.

A Welsh Songfest

Most of the early settlers in the Malad Valley were from Wales and until 1908 they had an annual celebration on St. David's Day, March 1. It was held in open air on a hilltop, with a chorus of not fewer than 180 voices, nor more than 200. The chief bard, chosen the year before, conducted the gathering, and called aloud, *A oes heddwch?* (Is there peace?) From the multitude came the answer, *Oes* (Yes). Then: "Chair the Bard," and the chosen one was conducted to a chair and received twenty pounds and was crowned. In Malad the event was a contest in various kinds of singing.

Rabbit Drives

Because of the fecundity and destructive ability of rabbits, drives were common formerly, and are still held now and then. Scores or hundreds of farmers, often with their wives and children, gathered and drove the rabbits into a corral and then clubbed them to death. Sometimes the screams could be heard for a mile. After the butchery, there was usually a withdrawal to refreshments, or more infrequently to a dance.

Postage[1]

This morning, Wells, Fargo and Co. put down the price of carrying letters to all parts of the U. S. to one bit a piece or ten cents where envelopes are bought in large quantities. Everybody can now write to his gal and enclose an envelope for an answer, all for two bits, no matter whether she be in Webfoot, Maine or New Orleans—everywhere within the limits of the Universal Yankee Nation; and creditors who expect no answers from their correspondents can dun for a bit. Mighty nice arrangement, this cheap postage.

Sagebrush

"I remember that sagebrush was 'legal tender.' Quite often a homesteader wishing to make a purchase would cut and trim a load of sagebrush and exchange it for what he needed."

Shopping

An old-timer in Silver City reminisces: Reticules were as fashionable in our day as now—only in our day they were quite a necessity because when we went shopping we had to carry gold dust in them. The storekeeper would weigh it out from our tiny chamois bags on scales made for that purpose. Calico was fifty cents a yard, muslin was a dollar. ... Yes, in Silver City in early days it was not unusual to have a party every night. One of the most popular dancing places was a butcher shop. We swept the sawdust out and danced around the hunks of meat.

"Socials"

The pie social was second to the dance in popularity, with women doing their best to make better pies than their neighbors. On one memorable occasion in an Idaho town, Grandma Blank received the honor. After listening to an evening of praise of her ability, and particularly of the fine job she did in crimping the crust, pride and elation so overcame the lady that she arose excitedly and announced that the crimping had been done with her set of new false teeth.

---

1 *Boise News*, Oct. 1, 1864, at Bannack City.

Fire Departments

In Coeur d'Alene: Our fire department consisted of a hand-drawn hose cart which when needed was manned by anyone who happened to be near, or by a team of horses if close at hand. The driver would hook on the hose cart, guess where the fire was, and speed away. Sometimes his guess was right and sometimes it was wrong. Maybe if he was lucky in his good intentions, the village boss would allow some compensation for speed in getting to the fire.

Speed Limits

Speed of various vehicles became so terrific in the early days of Coeur d'Alene that ordinances were passed and enforced to govern them. Neither bicycles nor horse-drawn contraptions were allowed to exceed eight miles an hour within the fire zone, or fifteen elsewhere in the city. Six miles an hour was the limit in turning a corner; four miles in passing from an alley into a street.

Schools

One room of the Oakley Meadows station was designated as the schoolhouse and the grain and hay, stored for the horses in one end of the room, were covered with sacks and pieces of burlap. The teacher's desk was a goods box, on which reposed one or two books, his one lead pencil, and the cowbell. The pupils sat in rows on backless benches, with the shorter legs dangling and the longer legs sprawled on the dirt floor. There was no blackboard but some of the pupils had slates, and there were a few pencils and sheets of brown paper. Lessons were, for the most part, oral; and penmanship was developed to the scratching rhythm of hard slate pencils on hard slates as the teacher counted, "one up—two down—three up—four down." There were only two classes, the "big" and the "little," and though some of the pupils were in fact big, there was little difference in the grade of work provided for them. The teacher was paid by subscriptions from the parents and other landholders.

Literary Societies[1]

In view of the long winter evenings that must intervene between now and spring, parties in town are about to resolve themselves into a literary society. We published a communication in relation to it last week and now call attention to it again in order that those who prefer spending their time in that way rather than in drinking saloons—the only places of public resort at present—may think of it, and, we hope, resolve in their own minds that it will be better not only for their mental but physical health, and a source of much more enjoyment to them to join an association of this kind that has for its object their advancement rather than to pursue a course that can only result in their debasement. We hope this may succeed.

Mail

When in the early eighties mail arrived at Eagle Rock, it was put into a box and anyone expecting or hoping for a letter ransacked through the whole pile.

Benefits of Female Society

In the Feb. 6, 1864, issue of the *Boise News,* a man declared the benefits of female society: It is better for you to pass an evening once or twice in a lady's drawing-room, even though the long conversation is slow, and you know the songs by heart, than in a club, tavern, or the pit of a theater. All amusements of youth to which virtuous women are not admitted are deleterious in their nature. All men who avoid female society have dull perceptions, and are stupid, or have gross tastes, and revolt against what is pure.

---

1 *Boise News,* Dec. 5, 1863

Your club swaggerers declare female society insipid. Poetry is insipid to a yokel; beauty has no charms for a blind man, music does not please a poor beast who does not know one tune from another. I protest that I can sit for a whole night talking to a well-regulated, kindly woman about her girl "coming out" or her boy at school, and like the evening's entertainment. One of the greatest benefits a man derives from woman's society is that he is bound to be respectful to them.

Our education makes us the most eminently selfish men in the world. We fight for ourselves, we perish for ourselves, we yawn for ourselves, we light our pipes for ourselves, and we prefer ourselves and our own ease—yet the greatest good that comes to man is from a woman's society for he has to think of somebody besides himself; somebody to whom he is bound to be constantly attentive and respectful.

Hospitality

It was the custom of miners in Idaho County to leave the latch-string out, to leave food in the cabin, and even gold dust on the table or shelves. Strangers often entered and stayed all night and departed, when the owner was away. Once a stranger accepted the hospitality, and on the next morning made off with all the gold dust in the cabin. He was overtaken and hanged the next day.

Ox Teams

A pioneer who was queried as to the practicality of oxen in early days, replied thus:

Were oxen satisfactory work animals? I liked them even to work on a farm. They moved slow but steady. They were gentle. When we got an animal that was hard to handle, we put him in the middle of several yokes of steers and he soon had to pull along like the rest of them. We used to leave a rope dragging when we turned the oxen loose. I don't believe their feet got as sore on the road as horses'. We did shoe them. The shoes were shaped like the steer's toes, with two shoes on each foot, one on each toe. The worst part about an ox team, you had to walk all the time to drive them.

Water Witches

In many areas the "diviner" was an important person. With a forked stick in his hands, the single shaft upward and each fork in his grasp, he walked back and forth to discover buried water or minerals. If the stick turned down in spite of him, it indicated water or ore, with the depth equal to the distance covered by the diviner between the point where the stick began to turn and the point where it pointed straight at the earth. Diviners still are in demand in certain parts of the State.

Lamps

When a lamp chimney broke the whole family would try to see what it looked like. Some broke in the form of a coffin, meaning a death; some in the form of a gold nugget, meaning wealth; but if it broke off at the circle at the base, that meant good luck or good health.

Utilities

In the early days of Coeur d'Alene, the water supply consisted of barrels of water hauled from the lake and sold at two bits a barrel delivered, with now and then a scooped-up fish for good measure. The lighting system was of table lamps, bracket lamps, and ceiling lamps, the brightness of each depending on the size of the wick, the quantity of kerosene, and the polish on the chimney. The telephone was a "tell-a-woman," and it is said by old-timers that the service was almost as rapid and efficient as any form of intercity communication of today.

Stables[1]

I have opened the old Establishment on a cash system. My long experience in the business renders it unnecessary to make any remarks in regard to the matter. My STABLE is LARGE & COMFORTABLE and I have also a LARGE CORRAL for WAGONS and TEAMS.

REMEMBER the old stand of Riggs & Agnew, corner Main and Seventh Streets, next door to Hart's Exchange, the

---

1 Idaho *Statesman*, March 2, 1867.

The Broken
Lamp Chimney

best hotel in Idaho Territory. Customers can have all and everything that they want except credit, and the first one that asks for it will get a cold shoulder, and the next one, two cold shoulders. I speak plain that I may be understood. —H. C. Riggs.

Grinding Grain

Two round stones about four feet in diameter and two feet thick were bolted together, with the insides corrugated. These two stones were turned in opposite directions; and though they did not touch, they were close enough to catch and crush the wheat. The crushed product was then sieved to separate the bran from the flour.

Domestic Help

In some communities it was customary to have Indian help. All the squaws were Mary and all the bucks were John. The Marys were good workers, especially at the family washing. The bucks did only as much as anyone by resourceful cunning could get out of them.

Sleighs

Those who could not afford to buy sleighs found trees with a natural crook and fashioned them into runners, using as shoes, not iron, which was expensive, but hardwood hewn to the proper shape. Sleighing parties were the chief winter diversion in many communities.

Currency

The Boise *Democrat* announced for Sept. 23, 1868: We are now situated so that no man in the country can say that he is too poor to take a newspaper. Bring along your truck —we'll take wood, vegetables, anything you have for subscriptions. If you want to read the *Democrat*, come and get it.

Hunting

The *Owyhee Avalanche* in 1866 reported a new way of hunting deer. The animals were maneuvered into deep snow and then pursued on snowshoes and knocked on the head. "This mode, we are told, is pretty successfully practiced during the snow season in this locality."

Pioneer Day

Pioneer Day commemorates the arrival of Brigham Young in the Salt Lake Valley. It is observed in many Mormon communities on July 24, and especially in such towns as Oakley, Rupert, Buhl, and others where it is an indispensable annual. In some places the men allow their beards to grow and have them trimmed after the fashion of nearly a century ago. Women dig into their trunks and fetch forth the old sunbonnets, bustles, parasols, pantalettes, ruffles, and furbelows that have been saved from generation to generation. The prairie schooner, ox cart, and stagecoach are sometimes used in the parades. The prospector may also enter, with pick and shovel roped to the side of a burro; and a wasp-waisted, high-bosomed damsel may ride a sidesaddle. But for the most part the celebration is one of usual rodeo events, with picnic and dance.

Diseases

For wolf-in-the-tail old-timers split the cow's tail open, poured salt and pepper into the wound and bandaged it up. I suppose they thought the "wolf" would sneeze himself to death.

"When a cow is sick and lies down, if you can keep her on her feet she will not die. So make a sling, wrap it around her and string her up with a derrick just high enough for her feet to touch the ground. If she dies, it will mean you did not get her up soon enough."

Dances

In the Boise *Democrat* for Sept. 23, 1868, a young man explained the quadrille: We both bowed to both of us, then together, then the fiddle tuned, and the thing started; grabbed her femail hand, she squeezed mine, we both slung each other but she slung the most because I think she loved me for a little while; then we changed base clear across the room, jumped up and over so many times, passed each other twice times, then my dear and I dosed a doe and hopped home again (from a foreign shore) ; then we two forward four, one ladies changed, we X over, turning around, twiced sash chayed sideways. I backed to place, she dittoed; side couples to the right, to the left, side couples tother way, side couples turn ladies, ladies turn side couples, gentlemen turn side couples, all hands round, back again, first feller take opposite side gal, sling her around and take your own gal and tother feller's gal forward and back, twist both gals twice times, sling 'em to opposite feller, let him do the same as you did, and back again to places, light gentlemen balance to heavy ladies, duplicate, promenade all, gals in the center, fellers get hold of each others hands, bob up and down, arms over the ladies' waterfalls, ladies stoop, jump up and down, each feller takes his gal back to place; right lady spin right gentleman, spin left gentleman, left gentleman spin left lady, all twist each other, do it over again, keep it up, all turn around, all turn the other, backward, sideways, each couple swing tother couple, cross over, back; all promenade to seats.

Miscellaneous

Many old-timers regarded coyote howling as very sweet music because it was believed that coyotes would not howl if there were any Indians in the neighborhood.

Women in early times preserved butter by putting it into a crock and pouring brine over it. Before using, the brine was poured off and the butter rinsed in cold water. The salt apparently affected it very little.

After the railroad shops were moved from Eagle Rock to Pocatello, citizens of the town gathered all the bedded and unrecovered ties and built their first sidewalk of them. It reached from the center of town to the armory, the amusement hall.

Pennies and nickels were an abomination to early storekeepers. Pennies they often refused; and nickels they threw into a bowl. After they had accumulated enough for a freight shipment, they sent them to San Francisco "to get rid of the pesky things."

In early days when doctors were scarce, it was a custom of many to put sulphur into their shoes to keep disease away. It is authentically reported that there are a few persons in Idaho today who still use sulphur for this purpose.

Pioneers, driving their mule teams across country, rode on the saddled back of the left mule nearest the first wagon, and handled all the reins from that position.

To prevent the rusting of tin, it was coated with lard when new and placed in a hot oven and heated thoroughly.

A half-and-half mixture of borax and white sugar was used to drive roaches away.

A raw potato was customarily used for a cover on the spout of a can.

Personal Reminiscences[1]

One way of making dye was to save the lye from the bed chamber and then put sage into it, of which the result was an indigo or navy blue. Wool was washed and corded, then spun into yarn and woven into cloth. Then the cloth was dyed. Sometimes to produce shades, skeins of yarn were wrapped tightly with cord and then dipped. When the skein was undone there were various shades in the color.

Ashes from wood and sagebrush were saved and then leached. This made lye water, which was used in home-made soap.

Worn-out dresses were used for petticoats. The worn or torn places were patched and then a thin layer of wool was quilted on. A hem at the bottom completed the job.

One popular game was blanket throwing. Eight persons would grasp a strong blanket and toss the person sitting on it. Though it seems to have been a rough game, it was not dangerous.

When I was six years old I went into the grain fields to gather straw for hats. The second joint of the straw was used because the first joint was too wet. How thrilled a person was in those days if he had a straw hat to wear!

---

[1] Mrs. E. B. Clark, of St. Anthony.

SOME CHINESE CUSTOMS

୶ଡ଼ଡ଼ୡ

Chinese Manners[1]

When a Chinese meets a friend on the street, instead of shaking hands with him he shakes with himself. If he walks with his friend, he deliberately keeps out of step, as to do otherwise would be bad manners. If they meet a third acquaintance, they are not rude enough to remove their hats; they do that in the approach, and in greeting put their hats back on. A Chinese eats his dessert at the beginning of a meal. If puzzled, he scratches not his head, but his foot. They do not consider it improper to refer to death; on the contrary, they cheerfully present their parents with coffins.

Chinese Burial Customs[2]

During the funerals, hundreds of pieces of brown paper, cut into small patterns with a hole in the center of each, were put into the casket of the dead person. It was supposed that the devil, if he sought the dead one, would have to seek his way through every one of these holes. Pieces of silver were also laid with the corpse so that the dead person could pay his journey through the spiritual realm. The money paid to wailers or to any other assisting was wrapped in red paper.

A Chinese Funeral[3]

The deceased was usually accompanied to his grave by a Chinese orchestra, which consisted of a gong (the sound of which was enough to wake the dead), reed instruments, and another instrument much like a banjo that had the wail of a coyote. Chinese women were hired to mourn; after smearing their faces with wet ashes, the wailing began and continued until it was defeated by the din of the orchestra. Twice a year the Chinese went out to feed their dead. Bowls of pork, rice, and whisky were set by the graves. On the following morning they noted with joy that the bowls were

1 As told in Silver City.
2 *Idem.*
3 *Idem.*

empty (coyotes got the pork, squirrels ate the rice, and white men took the whisky). After persons had been buried three years, one of the two Boise tongs sent men to exhume the bodies; whereupon the bones were taken apart, sealed in metal containers, and shipped for burial to the town in China were the person had been born.

Chinese Burial[1]

During a walk, last Sunday, we visited the graveyard, on the west side of Elk Creek, and witnessed a strange scene enacted there by a half-dozen Chinawomen, who were engaged in the ceremony of furnishing provisions to the dead celestials. Baked pork, fruits, apples, and rice were placed at the foot of one of the graves and a large number of wax tapers, joss sticks, and so forth, were lighted and placed around it. Cups of tea were then poured upon the ground, and an immense quantity of fancy paper was burnt. The women were laughing and apparently joking during this time, and occasionally they would prostrate themselves at the foot of the grave and bow their heads to the ground three or four times in succession. After going through with these performances, one of them deliberately pulled out her handkerchief, and, selecting a good seat on a box, she commenced singing, at the same time covering her face with her bandana. The song changed to wailing and crying in which all of them joined finally, and they kept up an unearthly din for about half an hour. We can hardly believe that their exhibitions of grief were genuine as we could see no trace of tears. They may have been hired mourners; and if so, that accounts for the businesslike manner in which they went at it.

Test of Guilt[2]

Quite a row occurred recently among the Chinese residents of this city occasioned by the "busting" of the Chinese Bank of Deposits, owned by the local members of the See Yup Company, and of which Eee Wood was one of the head officials.

About a week ago it was discovered that there was something rotten with the state of the bank and upon investiga-

1 From the *Idaho World*, April 20, 1871.
2 From the *Idaho World*, April 18, 1872.

tion, that practically all the funds had evaporated, to the extent of several thousand dollars of deposits and savings.

The greatest excitement prevailed in Chinatown. Criminations and recriminations were flung and reflung. Eee Wood was pounced upon as the guilty party, and his life was demanded for abusing the trust reposed in his honor and integrity. The bookkeeper was closely questioned, his accounts carefully examined, but nothing was found to implicate Eee Wood in the theft.

Finally the excited Chinamen decided to put him to the traditional test of guilt as prescribed by the doctrines of their religion. Accordingly, one day last week, all preparations being made beforehand, a delegation waited upon our worthy sheriff, Dryde McClintock, informing him that the ceremony was to take place at that time in the Chinese cemetery and requesting his presence there so that he could see "who shoot first."

By relieving those who were to attend the test, limited by Dryde to three of Eee's accusers, of their artillery, as well as the pruning knives found also on their persons, Dryde provided against any shooting at all before repairing with them to the cemetery.

There, the graves of defunct celestials were found lighted with wax tapers and decorated with slips of red paper holding prayers and messages for the dead. On a similar slip, in Chinese characters, the oath of innocence had been inscribed, placed on a grave, and fastened with small stakes. Eee Wood prostrated himself before this, rose, and bowed his head numerous times, then recited something in a singsong Chinese, probably the same oath, again prostrated himself, rose, seized a white rooster provided for the occasion, took a cleaver and severed its head.

Upon request, Sheriff McClintock dug a hole and buried the dead rooster, the cleaver and a paper slip bearing the oath of exculpation, for neither Eee Wood nor his erstwhile accusers would touch the sacrificial fowl nor the instrument of its destruction.

This ceremony is said to be of a very solemn nature with the Chinese, but it appears that in this instance it has not convinced all of them of Eee Wood's innocence. One of those who believe his oath was false was heard to say, "Me think he die velly soon."

The
Ka-ou-yit

INDIAN CUSTOMS

The Ka-ou-yit[1]

The Ka-ou-yit, celebrated annually by the Nez Perces of northern Idaho, has become a lively and complicated ceremony. This ritual grew out of the simple custom of giving thanks to the Great Spirit for supplying roots, fruits, and game for food. When the first roots of the spring had been gathered in and cooked, a family group seated in the wigwam would listen to a long recitation by their leader of the beginning of the earth and the coming of roots and other foods. A pot of porridge prepared from the roots was passed. The word itself designates the act of "eaten for the first time."

This feast gradually became first an occasion for family gatherings and finally an intertribal celebration. Elaborate dances and costumes now play a part in the festival; and relics such as tepees and the canoes used by Lewis and Clark

1 Based on an Indian account as recorded by R. G. Bailey, *River of No Return.*

The Ka-ou-yit.

are displayed. The event is the occasion of a great Indian
feast, with roots still playing an important part in the diet.
There are many visitors who come to witness this Indian
ceremony of thanksgiving.

Fort Hall Sun Dance

This, the most elaborate Indian ritual in Idaho, is held
annually in the latter part of July, in a small willow enclosure on top of a knoll about four miles west of the village
of Fort Hall. Originally the dance was a preparation for
war, and only those braves who had successfully withstood
the rigors of the dance and the ensuing contests were chosen
to avenge the tribal wrongs. Today, Indians ascribe health-
and strength-giving powers to the dance. For three days
the dancers moan songs to the rhythms of drums, chants
of onlookers, and the shrill cries of reed whistles. Periodic
rests are taken. At the conclusion of the dance, each participant is given a watermelon, his first nourishment for three
days. During the dance, a miniature tent city is pitched
near the entrance of the enclosure; and Indians in full
regalia from other reservations, as well as a great many
curious white persons, attend.

Horses and Firewater

Indians are said to have only two passions: horses and
whisky. Of the two, they have been more fastidious in
choosing the former, accepting in the latter anything that
had plenty of power in it. It could, indeed, be a hair tonic
or a cheap grade of vanilla flavoring. But horses have always
been a different matter: each buck takes pride in having the
fastest pony that could be bought, traded for, or stolen; and
at Indian meets in the past, the warriors not only wagered
the horses they were riding, but also all the other horses
they owned. The small lazy pintos were given to the squaws.
And possibly few peoples on the earth had such a whooping
good time as Indians when tribes got together for a celebration. The old bucks sat around drinking firewater while the
younger fellows raced and rode and finished up with a
bloodcurdling war dance.

Laundering

Indian women used the powdered formations around springs in the Soda Springs area for bleaching and cleaning leather, their robes and baby clothes, or anything else which they wished to whiten.

Rearing Children

"Their children (at Fort Hall) seem to grow up practically without restraints, and to be happy in this freedom; yet they obey quickly when called on to do so. And what they enjoy they enjoy completely and freely and without compunction or question."

Social Life

On the Fort Hall Reservation, social activities are limited almost entirely to visiting, dancing, and gambling. On almost any evening, the Indians can be seen congregated around the lodges, gambling and playing games, of which the most popular is the stick game.

Headdress

Unmarried Indian women wear a feather headdress similar to that worn by Indian men, save that it is less elaborate and the feathers are shorter. One long feather, pointing up, is fastened at the back of the head. Married women wear kerchiefs tied over their heads, usually bright-colored, flowered, embroidered, or designed in gay and contrasting colors.

Music

Among Fort Hall Indians there is worship by functions, rituals, and songs. The traditional music of the tribes has survived and can still be heard at dances and other festivals; nor has the cry of the coyote been taken out of this music. For did not the coyote sing when he discovered and destroyed the obsidian mountain whence came arrow points and spears, which caused suffering and death? Did he not stealthily approach from behind and push the mountain over, scattering fragments everywhere? Those who heard his song and learned it, sing as he sang; for the cry of the coyote is still a part of Indian song.

Prayer Bags

Each Indian has his own "medicine" or prayer bag. At the age of fifteen the boy enters a period of meditation and communication with the Great Spirit. During this he has a dream and in it sees certain animals, which, he is certain, hold for him some special significance as a guide through life. Thereupon he learns what he can of the animals or birds which he has seen in his vision, and makes a collection of small precious things which, wrapped in a piece of hide, constitute his prayer bag, his "bundle of powerful medicine." He now makes his medicine vows, to which he must remain faithful throughout his life; to be false to them would be comparable to a white man's being faithless to his society or his God.

Religion

Some of the better-educated Indians who have read the Book of Mormon declare that there are notable similarities between its history and doctrines and those of the Indians; but Indians today, as formerly, are baptized into whatever Christian sect is handiest. An effort is made on the reservations in Idaho to make Christians of the Indians; but as an old Bannack at Fort Hall says, "You can still lead a horse to water but—" Some who know Indians well declare it is a grave mistake to confuse them with the intricate perplexities of the white man's religion, and to lead them away from their own beliefs, which for them are so simple and understandable.

Burial

When an Indian dies, relatives gather to assist in the rites and the mourning; and if the family is willing to make gifts of calico, horses, or money, many visitors are likely to be on hand. The wailing for the dead one continues as long as the mourners can keep it up, or as long as the body can be kept in a state of preservation. Before gifts are placed in the grave, they are held up to view; and if anyone present de-

sires any of the articles, he has only to claim it. This practice, however, is regarded as unethical, and greed seldom
makes demands. There are those who say the Bannacks and
Shoshonis never buried their dead in treetops; others, who
assume to be as well informed, declare that they did.

It is reported that among some Idaho Indians today the
body is recovered after a Christian burial and wrapped in
a silk shawl and a blanket. A large twig, covered with
thorns, is placed in the right hand of the corpse to ward
off evil spirits.

Caste

There is evidence of class distinctions among the Indians
on the Fort Hall Reservation. The Shoshonis, perhaps because more numerous, seem to be the aristocrats, a circumstance deeply resented by the proud and pure-blooded Bannacks. The half-breeds, chiefly of French-Indian blood,
are looked down upon by both tribes. They are regarded
as troublemakers, possibly in part because they are better
educated, better mannered, and have more sympathy for the
ways of white folk. The half-breed is quite pathetic: a man
without a country who has no voice in tribal affairs.

Hot Baths[1]

Steam baths or sweathouses were used for the purpose
of purification in Nez Perce religious rites. These sweathouses usually consisted of a hole in the ground, from three
to eight feet deep and about fifteen feet in diameter, a small
hole being left for entrance and the same having been
closed after the bather entered. In this ovenlike receptacle,
heated to a suffocating temperature, the naked native wal-
lowed in the steam and mud, singing, yelling, and praying;
and at last he rushed forth dripping with perspiration and
plunged into the nearest stream.

As Craftsmen

Southern Idaho Indian women were hard workers, tan-
ning the skins, making most of the gloves and baskets which
were sold to the whites. They did the sewing for the
family, and their skill remains an astounding fact to me.
I have watched a squaw take a piece of calico and with
never a sign of a pattern, fashion out of it a close-fitting
dress or jacket merely by looking at her customer as she
cut the full-length pieces. I have asked to see the pattern for
intricate beadwork on gloves and moccasins, but Nellie or
Maggie or Mary would say that "Out-of-doors, he make-um
pattern," and with a giggle go right on building flowers and
birds, stars and crowns, out of the magic of yellow and blue
and red and green beads.

Healers

Among Indians, only a chosen few had the power of
healing, and each of these had his own pipe manager.
When a person became ill, his relatives notified the pipe
manager of the healer wanted, and the time to come. When
the healer came to the sick person's tent, he found him
sitting facing the west, with a fire burning in the center of
the tepee. The healer slowly circled this fire, chanting as he
went, until he felt the power of healing coming into his body;
whereupon this power enabled him to see through the body
of the sick person and to locate the pain. He then placed
his right hand on the spot where he saw sickness and drew

---

1 From Hiram T. French, *History of Idaho.*

the sickness out and into his own hand and thence into his mouth. He swallowed it and then spit it out, so ridding the ill one of the germ or bug that caused the sickness. The healer's pipe manager, sitting just inside the door, then filled and lighted a pipe and handed it to the healer, who took a puff and passed it to the relatives. The healer was given a fee in horses, money, or calico; but if his patient died, this fee was to be returned.

Polygamy

The *Idaho World* of Sept. 24, 1883, reports that the ceremony of receiving Sitting Bull had to be postponed because he could not make up his mind which of his wives he would let go. The tenets of the Catholic Church forbade a communicant more than one wife. Bishop Morley had been giving him religious instruction for several months and the old war chief was ready for confirmation—but separation from his various wives proved too much for him, and he would probably revert to heathenism.

As Bronco Busters

Indian braves were not bronco busters. They filled two slender sacks with sand and tied them together and threw them astride the cayuse. They encouraged lusty bucking by putting a rope around the beast's flanks and hanging on to the end of it at a safe distance from the flying heels. When the pony was exhausted, then a warrior mounted. Another practice was to starve the horse until he was almost too weak to stand; whereupon the brave mounted him and starved him by turns until the animal was broken.

Indian Craps

A basket was used of about twelve to twenty inches in diameter. Pieces of bone or crockery, each about the size of a quarter, with numbers on them were placed in the basket. The basket was shaken and the numbers read; the score was kept with sticks.

Arrow Pitching

A favorite pastime was arrow pitching, with two or three men on each side. An arrow was thrown so that it stuck up in the earth about two hundred feet away. Each contestant threw arrows as close to the first one as he could.

Just Plain Indian

One Indian family has moved about a great deal from one reservation to another. There are six children. Four of them have been baptized in five different Protestant sects, but at heart they are still just plain Indian, with their old beliefs and superstitions.

Harvest Prayer

Each harvest was preceded by a ceremony which included a prayer of thanksgiving and an offering of the first fruit of the season, followed by a harvest dance. The prayer and offering by the chief were directed toward the highest mountain within sight.

Whistles and Drums

Whistles were often made from the wing bones of the eagle. Drums were of two sizes: the small head drums covered on one side with horsehide or cowhide, and tied on the other with thongs; and the large drums fashioned from a hollowed section of a tree and covered with elkhide on the ends. The covers were decorated. The larger drums had four loops, allowing suspension of the drums from pegs driven into the earth.

Liars

According to Nez Perce standards, lying was the worst of crimes, and the liar was placed under every form of insult that the Indian could think of. For adultery, death was sometimes the punishment, depending upon the attitude of the man to whom the offending woman belonged. For stealing, the worst punishment was the forced return of the stolen goods. Murder was not regarded as a crime, though to kill a guest was a breach of hospitality.

Food Today and Yesterday

Indian foods today are chiefly those of the white man: they are especially fond of doughnuts, bananas, and ice cream. Formerly, the more civilized tribes in Idaho lived chiefly on wild meats, fish, berries, and roots; but those of inferior tribes ate great quantities of snakes and mice.

The old Indians prefer to boil or roast meats over a campfire, using very little salt, and to bake unleavened bread in hot ashes or a Dutch oven. Berry and seed grinders of stone are still in use. Any surplus meat is dried and made into pemmican as it was ages ago; but there is very little surplus now!

Their mode of dressing salmon is simple and good. They take out all the bones and much of the flesh, and then stretch the skin on crossed sticks and broil it over a slow fire. This process is said to preserve the flavor.

Because of the devastation of sheep, Indian foods do not for the most part mature as formerly, especially roots, seeds, and bulbs. Indians still gather wild berries, especially chokecherries, serviceberries, gooseberries, and currants. These are dried by the older women, canned by the younger ones. The older people always use baskets for the gathering of sunflower seeds or grains. They dry the roots they get from Camas Prairie, and crush or grind their chokecherries.

In preparation for the smoking of fish, Indians built a long trough of rocks and mud about a foot and a half high, with one end built up so there would be a draft of air. The fish were split down the spine, dipped in salt water, and laid on willows. The smudge was kept going until the fish were superbly smoked.

There were always some Indians on Rock Creek, for the stream was plentifully supplied with fish, and a goodly supply of rabbits and cottontails was to be found on the hillsides. Every autumn members of the tribe would gather near the mouth of Rock Creek for a salmon hunt. Great quantities of fish were speared, dried, and smoked for winter use, and then often used as exchange in payment of gambling debts incurred while the women of the tribe were

Fishing

busy with curing of the catch. After the salmon run was over, the Indians moved up on Camas Prairie near Fairfield to dig camas roots and trade blankets, horses, buffalo robes, fish, and squaws. When winter came, many of them went back to the reservation to live with Uncle Sam, because, as one old fellow said, "He got-um heap meat and flour."

In former times, a favorite method of catching fish was to create eddies in streams by means of dams. When the fish reached the eddies they paused to rest, whereupon the Indians speared them.

There seem to have been two kinds of camas root, one of which, resembling an artichoke in shape, was dried and pounded into flour and baked into bread. Old-timers who ate the bread declare that it was like nothing so much as a mouthful of brown wrapping paper. The other root, the onion camas, so called because of its shape, was dried but not pulverized. It was used as a kind of confection because it has a flavor much like that of licorice.

Miscellaneous

Along the Lolo Trail was in former times a favorite hunting and fishing area for Indians. Under a certain rock, known only to them, and today called the Indian Post Office, the hunters left news of their success as well as of the better hunting grounds for those who came after. Under the rock they stored grass, so that the next hunters would know by the withering how long it had been since the messages were left. A little beyond is a pile of rocks known as the Hee Hee Stand. This was a spot of worship for the Nez Perce Indians; and Sacajawea herself, it is said, rested and prayed here when journeying westward with Lewis and Clark.

In 1873, when goods were still freighted into Pierce City from Lewiston over difficult trails, an Indian offered for sale his beautiful daughter. The first white man bid fifty cents, the second $3.50 plus two deer hides; but the third offered the incredible price of two fishhooks and won. He married her and they had five children and later moved to the vicinity of Kendrick, where the woman and children each received eighty acres of land from the Federal Government, and the husband, ineligible for such a gift, became manager. Their descendants still live on the original homesteads.

Among the Nez Perces fatigue was overcome by a ceremony which was supposed to confer endurance on the participant. It consisted of thrusting willow sticks down the throat and into the stomach, a succession of hot and cold baths, and fasting.

When the Pend d'Oreille Indians were reduced to severe straits, they buried the old and the very young alive, declaring that neither was able to care for himself.

Indian babies were usually born by running streams and immediately dipped into cold water. White women thought it a cruel practice and protested; but the Indians only laughed and said, "When-um git big can eat everything, no git-um bellyache like paleface."

When the Halley sisters came to Idaho in a wagon train, Indians wanted to trade a beautiful white horse for the younger girl.

Shoshoni means "abundance of grass." The Shoshonis used to braid horse hair in with their own to indicate the tribe to which they belonged.

Formerly, among the Bannacks, an Indian brave would hold up one hand to indicate he was an enemy, two to show that he was without weapons and a friend.

The primitive Indian dog was a coyote that had been selected, bred up, and domesticated.

In the matter of property rights, the Nez Perces were progressive, all family possessions reverting to the man in the event of a separation. Slavery practiced among them was like that in other tribes; namely, the right of life and death over prisoners of war. These Indians, however, treated their slaves well, often taking them into the tribe.

~

At the Lapwai Mission in the thirties, Indian children formed a bucket brigade and thereby kept moist the precious seedlings of the first fruit trees planted in the State.

~

In times of peace, the Nez Perce Indians isolated themselves in village groups. Each band had in addition to its village a fishing place and a strip of land along the river. Boundaries were established by mutual consent of neighboring groups.

A Sun Dance at Buffalo Lodge

Buffalo Lodge, a willow-enclosed arena surrounded by tepees placed at regular intervals of approximately a hundred yards, is located in the heart of the desert not far from Fort Hall.

The "God-Pole," a tall forked pole, was placed in the center of the arena, and topped with colored banners. The pole was said to represent the figure of Christ and the Crucifixion; twelve other poles represented the twelve apostles. There was a small bundle of willow twigs in which the spirit of the Sun God was said to dwell and listen to the pleas of the dancers. Near the center of the pole was placed the head of a buffalo, representing the king and the highest in beasts. A little above the buffalo head was the eagle.

The sun had long since gone down behind the Lost River Mountains when the call came for the dancers to start. The parade started from the tepees. Upon reaching the arena the Indians circled the outside once and broke into two formations, one going one way, the other formation going the opposite. The formations circled the arena once again and entered it through the only entrance, that on the east side. The musicians then took their places along the sides of the enclosure. Alex Woods, acting as taskmaster or master of ceremonies, took his place, his back resting against the God-Pole and facing the west, right arm upraised, and began the prayer. The prayer lasted twenty minutes, and then the dance began.

An aged Indian, suffering from paralysis, was led forward. He placed his hands on the God-Pole while the taskmaster, placing his hands upon him, asked a blessing upon him. Some of his relatives were dancing for the aged Indian. Sometimes in twos and threes and sometimes singly, the dancers advanced back and forth to and from the pole, blowing their eagle whistles to the accompaniment of the tomtoms. Along about two or three o'clock in the morning the dance took on an eerie and more barbaric significance. The most impressive part of the ceremony took place at dawn. Facing the east now, instead of the west, the medicine men began their own special services. The women were allowed in the arena in the early morning hours. All during this eighty-hour period the Indians danced in their bare feet, naked to the waist, their blankets placed where they could be reached if needed.

After the dance was over and the dancers were sufficiently rested, the feast began. It consisted mostly of barbecued buffalo meat and watermelon.

Many tribes were represented at this gathering. Old bucks with their hair in braids, young bucks with the latest in haircuts and brilliantly colored shirts, old squaws with their colored shawls, and young married moderns carrying their papooses in their arms instead of on their backs; in cars they came, in wagons, and on horseback.

Ceremonial of Ancient Origin

The Dance of the Sun originated so long ago that there is no record of its beginning. It was a prayer for health and strength and a strange mixture of the teachings of Christianity and the practices of ancient barbarism.

Originally a dance of torture, it is said that the Sun Dance was also a war dance by means of which the leaders of war parties were selected, a sort of contest of endurance among the young braves of the various tribes. Each dancer was compelled to cut a deep gash through the fleshy part of his breast or shoulders; and through this gash a strip of green buffalo hide was tied and the other end was fastened to the pole in the center of the group of dancers. As the participants danced to and fro, back and forth to the pole, they struggled to break either the buffalo hide or their own flesh where the hide was tied. The chiefs were chosen from among those who first succeeded in freeing themselves. But this practice, of course, has long since ceased, and the dance has become actually a religious rite and a medicine dance.

The blind, the aged, and the crippled come to the willow-enclosed arena with the most implicit faith that the Great Spirit who has now come to dwell within the enclosure will grant them relief from their suffering and ills; and with this discard their crutches and dance as the others; the stooped become erect and bandages are torn from tired old eyes, half blinded by cataracts. There is no doubt that many cures are effected by the Indian's faith and the power of will to overcome his own infirmities. And there is no doubt in the minds of medical men that abstinence from food and drink, together with the excessive perspiration caused by the exercise, helps to expel many of the poisons from their bodies and to improve their physical condition.

Smoking is allowed and practiced during the dance, but no food or water is taken. Those who wish to join in the dance have until midnight of the first night to do so; but once a person has joined, he is not allowed to drop out lest he break the blessing for all the participants. He must go on until the end of the eighty-hour period, or, if he faints, he is allowed to lie as he fell until he becomes conscious. The young braves often dance for the relatives who are too old or too infirm to participate. Brief intervals of rest are allowed, but while some rest, others must dance.

The Stick Game

This old Indian game was played among the Western tribes. Nearly always in the evening when the other forms of sport had ceased for the night the men, taking sides, would seat themselves on the ground opposite each other in a long straight line with a wooden pole on the ground between the lines. A long time would be spent in betting, and each would take a good look at the one making the bet, and although no books were kept, no names recorded, mistakes were seldom made. They seemed to remember every bet and who made it.

After all the available bets seemed to be placed the game

was made ready to start and each side took ten sticks about eight or ten inches long, sharpened at one end to stick in the ground. Then there was a flip for heads or tails. When the winner of the guess was ready, a small piece of bone about two and one-half inches long and one-half inch in diameter was produced, and the luckiest Indian was chosen to hide the bone in his two hands. During the hiding or trying to hide the bone, the whole line of Indians on his side sang, shouted, and pounded on the pole with sticks. In fact, a terrible racket was carried on until the man hiding the bone was ready to hold out his hands for the other side to guess. Then there was much whispering, grunting, and low talking; and after deliberation the old Indian in the center of the line touched the hand he thought the bone was in. If he was right, his side then received the bone and the other side did some guessing; if he was wrong, his side lost a stick to the other side.

The object of the game was for one side or the other to get all the sticks and win all bets. The game, though simple, sometimes consumed a whole night and part of the next day as first one side and then the other ran into luck. The squaws played the game by themselves at some distance from the men.

Life for a Life

Whether Indians believed and practiced faithfully without exception, as part of their religious custom, the law of "a life for a life" seems not to be known, but there are several well-known instances that indicate they did.

Panguedge, an Indian scout, who had won the respect and gratitude of the early settlers of Owyhee County for his aid during the Indian wars, forfeited his life. As he began to age and became impatient and cranky, he had an argument with the son of a worthless renegade tribesman, and he struck the child on the head and accidentally killed him. It was necessary, according to tribal rites, for Panguedge to be killed. He was said to have been a fine-looking Indian well over six feet tall and weighing about two hundred pounds. He spoke English excellently.

There was also the case of the wife of old Chief Winnemucca. The old chief was well liked among the people in the vicinity, and his passing was much regretted by the white settlers as well as by the Indians. After his burial his wife was stoned to death. She was placed in the center of a circle of Indians who held rocks in their hands and was thereupon stoned until pronounced dead.

Stoning the Widow.

Superstitions

RUNYAN

Signs and Portents

It is a sign of rain if:
1. The new moon is tipped so that water will run out of it;
2. The leaves of the silver poplar turn bottomside up;
3. A dog sleeps on his back with his feet in the air;
4. Soot burns inside a stove.

It is a sign of approaching storm if:
1. There are circles around the sun (and some say the moon);
2. Horses run around and snort and hold their heads high;
3. Crickets chirp loudly and persistently;
4. Coyotes howl or owls hoot;
5. A flock of domestic geese follow a leader; but if they scatter and refuse to remain in groups, fair weather is ahead.

Weather Signs.

A whirlwind portends a dry spell, the size of the wind declaring the duration of the drouth. If chickens remain out in a rain, it will be only a brief shower. If the sun shines during a rain, there will be rain on the following day.

It is a sign of cold weather if:
1. Wild ducks fly southward;
2. The moon is far in the north.

It is a sign of an early fall if:
1. Many caterpillars are seen crawling over the ground.

It is a sign of a hard winter if:
1. Pine squirrels leave the hills and come down to ranches in the valleys;
2. Chipmunks, squirrels, or beaver store a large abundance of food;
3. The muskrat builds an unusually large mound;
4. Weeds grow very tall;
5. Wild birds or beasts grow a heavier coat of feathers or fur;
6. There is a heavy layer of dead leaves on the ground from the last summer's growth;
7. The milt of a butchered hog is thick at the upper end. If the milt is long and slender, the winter will be long and mild.

An Idahoan reports: A cat is weatherwise. When mine bathes herself, I pack my lunch, lace my boots and take to the hills, knowing the weather will be fine. If she licks her fur the wrong way or washes herself over her ears or sits with her tail to the fire, then I know a storm is coming.

Dark of the Moon Calf.

If a calf is taken from a cow during the dark of the moon, the mother will never grieve over the loss.

If in sewing a garment, three needles are broken, the person who wears the garment will not outlive it.

Stepping across a dead animal means ten years of bad luck. It also portends bad luck if (1) you iron the back of a shirt; if (2) you sweep after dark; if (3) you pass salt at a table: set the shaker down and let the next person pick it up; if (4) you sing in bed or open an umbrella in the house or put a garment on wrong side out or hear a rooster crowing in the night or swing a chair around on its legs or leave your bed left foot first or enter a house by one door and leave by another.

It is a sign of death for you or another if you sneeze three times in succession; if a rocking chair rocks with nobody in it; if a wild bird enters a house; if a dog howls (especially under a window) in the night; or if a bird sings under or on a window ledge. If you sweep under a sick person's bed, he will die, as he will also if a dog crawls under his bed.

"My grandmother used to say that every stitch you sewed on Sunday you would have to pick out with your nose when you went to heaven."

Indians planted fish in each hill of corn, not knowing that the good luck lay in the fertilizer.

If you trim your fingernails on Sunday you will be ill during the following week.

To throw bread into your fire will bring want to your door.

To dream of a wedding foretells death; of snakes, enemies; of the dead, news of the living. If you dream the same dream three nights in a row, it will come true.

Seven Portents
of Death

Big ears indicate generosity, small ears, stinginess; eyes too close together mean cupidity, a huge nose declares sexual precocity, and a retreating chin indicates weakness of purpose.

A hog butchered in the light of the moon yields more lard than when killed in the dark of the moon.

A green Christmas means a fat graveyard. Sick persons usually die in the spring when petals fall, or in the autumn when leaves fall.

To make flowers bloom profusely, water them frequently with fresh blood.

If you want a golden tooth, feed the extracted tooth to a chicken. Among many old-timers it was believed that a baby's tooth when extracted should be buried; for if it was found and eaten by a dog or a coyote or pig, the child would have a tooth like that of the beast which had eaten the first one. Some parents still believe this to be the cause of unsightly tusks.

If a person enters a house when a woman is churning, she should at once work the dasher up and down a few times or the butter will spoil.

If two friends separate and walk on two sides of an obstruction (such as a person or a fallen tree), they will soon have a fight.

A mole on your forehead means good fortune; but an itching nose declares that you are going to kiss a fool. If you scratch your nose on the right side, a man is coming; if on the left, a woman.

If you have chills down your spine, someone is walking across the spot where your grave will be.

If you drop a dishrag, the act portends the arrival of someone dirtier than yourself.

Among Indians, amulets of various kinds are worn, including spruce needles, which are placed in a buckskin bag and carried around the neck. A weasel foot worn on the hat of a warrior aids him in catching a squaw. Among whites, the commonest charm against evil or illness seems to be a small sack of asafetida carried from the neck. When superstitious Chinese go to bed, they arrange their shoes so that one points in one direction and the other in the opposite direction. If shoes are arranged so, the devil will not be able to track them through their dreams.

Chinese also believe that if a member of their race dies with his eyes open, the circumstance foretells disaster. When Ah Lee, the old water carrier, died in Silver City with his eyes open there was great consternation; nor was it allayed when a considerate observer pointed out that at least he had died with his mouth shut. A short while later, news came of the San Francisco earthquake, and the message in the open eyes was fulfilled.

Indians also effected a charm against evil by placing a rattlesnake's head on hot coals in a hole in the earth and covering it with fresh liver and gall of wild beasts. During the steaming, the liver absorbs the poison from the head, and the head is then worn in a buckskin bag. Some of the older Indian women carry pieces of obsidian to ward off disease; and some of the older men carry spears of grass. An Indian love charm was the root of the bloodroot plant, the juice of which the lover smeared on his palm; whereupon he extended to the maiden his hand, palm turned upward, and within a few days she became his bride.

Jelly made in moonlight jells hard.

The Coeur d'Alene Indians refused to enter the waters of Hayden Lake because, they said, one of their tribe had been drowned there and never recovered therefrom. This lake has no outlet; the body of the drowned man was found in Lake Coeur d'Alene.

A character in Greenwood's *We Sagebrush Folks* declares: "The reason a hog dies from running in the heat is that the lard in it melts and runs around inside, clogging up its innards."

Shoshoni Indians believe it is unlucky to tell stories during the day; and if stories are told of the coyote at any time, rainy or cold weather will follow.

Chinese believe that if a person does not die in his own house, bad luck will come to the owner of the house in which the person dies.

Formerly, when certain Indian tribes desired rain, they killed a frog with a stone and laid it on its back.

When you hear the first cricket in the fall, it is just six weeks until the first frost.

The Shoshonis dread ghosts and avoid passing cemeteries at night. Nevertheless, meetings with ghosts are frequent. Jack Grouse, for instance, heard singing and then saw a female figure: the next spring his father died. Another Indian met a very insolent and ill-mannered ghost who tried to push him over by assaulting him from behind. The warrior struggled to catch hold of a bare rib; and though he did not, he did become very strong, and thereafter lifted horses for the fun of it. If an Indian is fortunate enough to give a ghost the worst of it, he becomes a mighty warrior thereafter.

In the Malad Valley many years ago lived a woman who would throw cream to the hogs if butter did not come when she thought it should. She declared the cream was bewitched. One day she was seen beating the daylights out of a calf; and when asked what she was doing, she retorted that she was knocking the witches out of it.

When wheat is planted in the light of the moon it does not have smut. Potatoes and beets ought to be planted in the dark of the moon, but all things that grow above ground demand the light of the moon for planting.

Rain on Easter Sunday portends rain for seven consecutive Sundays.

I never believed in witches, but when a little girl I visited my grandmother. She lived in a large house and had a new maid who was upstairs. A cat came down the stairway howling and clawing and rolling over and over. My grand-

mother said, "There now, that girl has bewitched the cat!"
I went upstairs and asked the girl how she had done it. She
said she wondered if turpentine was good for cats, so she had
given the creature a large dose.

〜

Some women won't set hens in June, believing it is a
bad month for hatching, and others declare that thunder
kills chicks in the shells.   〜

> If in July, friend, you wed,
> You'll always labor for your bread.
> If you buy a broom in May,
> You'll sweep your relatives away.

〜

When sleeping out in the open, put a hair rope around
your bed to keep snakes away; and if you want it to rain
before sundown, go kill a spider.

〜

If you cannot start a fire that will burn readily, you will
have a lazy husband.   〜

If you want your wish to come true, make it before a
falling star disappears. If that does not work, burn an old
pair of shoes. If you wish to see or dream of or meet your
future mate:

1. Eat a thimbleful of salt and walk backwards to your
   bed; or
2. Strike a match and hold it straight up until it burns
   your finger. The charred staff will bend in the direction of your future mate's home; or
3. Find nine peas in a pod and place the pod over the
   door, and the first person who enters will be your husband or wife; or
4. Sleep on Halloween night with a perfect peeling of an
   apple under your pillow and you will dream of him
   or her; or
5. Break a wishbone and hang your part above the door
   and wait for the first person to walk under it; or
6. Drop a cherry into a glass of water: if within twenty-
   four hours it does not sink, you will soon meet your
   mate. If the cherry sinks, try another; or

7. Put one grain of salt into a teaspoonful of water and swallow just before going to bed, and your dream will advise you. If none of these work, you might try the plot of a girl who was successful:
8. A girl named the four corners of her bedroom for a different man, slept on her stomach, and as a result dreamed of the man she was to marry. This always works.

Folk Medicine

Abscess: A paste of ground charcoal mixed with homemade yeast was used by women to rub on their breasts while nursing, as well as for a poultice for abscessed lungs.

Aches: Among many cures was brown paper applied after it had been soaked in vinegar and pepper.

Aching teeth: All kinds of things have been put into aching teeth, but the most potent is perhaps carbolic acid, for it destroys the nerve and kills the ache. A woman in Nicholia put lye into a decayed tooth and lost the use of one arm.

Appendicitis: Kill a black cat on a night when there is a full moon, split the cat down his spine, and apply the warm organs to the pain.

Baby's eyes: An old custom was to wash the newborn babe's eyes with milk from its mother's breast.

Bed-wetting: Cook a mouse, preferably by boiling, and make the flesh into a sandwich and feed to the child.

Bleeding: Among the many cures for bleeding were the ashes of burned rags. Many frontiersmen in Idaho used the sap of spruce trees and found it effective. The *Idaho World* reported in 1865 the following: A friend tells us that he cut his foot with an axe. The lady of the house seized his foot and held it over a pan containing smoking tag locks (wool). In a few minutes the bleeding stopped; the smoking pan was removed, and the wound healed in a remarkably short time.

Blood tonics: The roots and bark and leaves of many plants were steeped for tonics. Among the commonest were sagebrush, yarrow, wild graperoot, and the bark of the aspen. Often the teas of many roots and barks were

mixed, and it was sometimes thought that the more
bitter the liquid, the more effective it would be.

Bloat: For bloat in cattle, tie a rope around the tongue and
lower jaw and twist it firmly. This is said to cause belch-
ing and to bring relief.

Boils: To draw a boil to a head, cover it with the membrane
from the inside of an eggshell. To kill a boil, apply
turpentine generously and often. Many sorts of poultices
were used, a favorite material being common mud.

Burns: Apply a poultice of tea leaves and raw potato; or of
slippery elm bark with enough water to thicken; or of
balsam juice (a favorite with the Indians) ; or of a
mixture of grated potato and soda. If these fail, hold
the injured part in the dense smoke from burning wool
or woolen rags. Perhaps commonest of all remedies is
a simple poultice of baking soda.

Cancer: An old-timer declares that a cancer can be healed
with an application of cobwebs.

Canker: Among pioneers doubtless the commonest (and a
very effective) cure for canker was black gunpowder
held in the mouth and dissolved against the sores. Another remedy was a syrup of sage leaves, powdered alum,
golden seal, and honey. It was taken internally and a
teaspoonful is a dose.

Chilblains: Undoubtedly the best cure is a walk of about
two hundred yards barefooted in the snow. Other cures
are an application of a paste of gunpowder and lard;
the holding of the feet in the smoke of burning cornmeal;
or soaking the feet in warm water to which horse dung
has been added. Various kinds of dung figure promi-
nently in many old-time remedies.

Colds: Many are the cures for the ailment which still baffles
medical science. Here are a few of the many that have
been reported. Poultices to the chest: goose grease and
onion juice; lard, peppermint, turpentine, and kerosene
heated and rubbed in; a pint of vinegar, a slice of bacon
and a goodly amount of black pepper; a teaspoonful of
melted lard, one of turpentine and two of kerosene applied to both chest and back; a package of fine cut
tobacco, a package of raisins and a cup of lard cooked
together, to which, when cool, is added a large spoon of
boric acid. To take internally: a few drops of turpentine

Bloat

in sugar; a glass of hot water to which has been added the juice of two lemons and enough soda to cause a generous exhalation of bubbles; a glass of hot milk (a Basque remedy) to which has been added a third of a glass of whisky and a teaspoon of sugar; rock candy dissolved in whisky; a sirup of onions. Another: heat a half tub of water and have the patient sit on a table leaf across the tub with his feet in a bucket of hot mustard water. Wrap him in a heavy blanket and let him steam while his feet soak, and fill him with hot ginger tea to encourage sweating. After the ordeal, rub him with hot oil and put him to bed. For croup, apply to the throat a mixture of two parts vinegar, one part turpentine, and a well-beaten egg. Perhaps better, at least in desperate cases, is a half-teaspoonful of kerosene taken internally. An Indian remedy was boiled camas root.

Colic: Into a saucer of milk blow tobacco smoke and then feed the milk to the baby.

Consumption: The following cure was reported by the *Idaho World,* Oct. 18, 1878: The flower of the mullein plant made into strong tea, sweetened with sugar and taken freely has cured a number of cases. The medicine must be continued from three to six months. It is very good for the blood vessels also. It makes good blood and takes inflammation from the lungs.

Coughs: The *Idaho World,* Dec. 3, 1864: The remedy I propose has been tried by me and recommended to others with good results. Take into the stomach before retiring a piece of raw onion. It tends to collect the water from the lungs and throat, causing instant relief.

This gentleman, however, also declares that it is excellent to apply raw onion to the armpits to draw poisons from the body. Another remedy: Mix one pint of strained honey, one tablespoon of cream of tartar, and the juice of two lemons. Dose: a teaspoonful every hour until relieved. Another old-timer reports that skunk grease is fine, but did not say whether it is to be taken internally or applied. Some pioneers took nearly everything into their stomachs.

Cure-alls: A popular Chinese cure-all is dried and pulverized horned toads; another is the flesh of skunks dried in the sun; and a third is rice whisky. Whites who have tried the last have, it is said, got down and prayed to die. A common cure-all is tea made of peach-tree leaves. To keep diseases away, boil water to which has been added a generous quantity of carbolic acid. A cure-all liniment is wormwood tea.

Cuts: Apply a poultice of sugar soaked in turpentine; or the juice of the spruce tree; or a juicy quid of chewing tobacco; or grated nutmeg. For healing, make a salve of witch hazel and arsenic.

Dandruff: There seems little doubt that sagebrush tea is excellent for the hair and scalp. The leaves only should be used, and these ought to be gathered when green. After they are steeped, the tea can be used as a shampoo, and several rinsings in cold water will destroy the odor. Scores of Idahoans sent in this simple remedy to cure dandruff and promote the growth and luster of hair.

Delirium tremens: Give red pepper in doses of sixty grains at a time. It effects a cure in a few hours.

Diphtheria: An old remedy was salt pork heated very hot and applied to the throat. It is said that it draws out the poison and forms large blisters under the skin which were lanced if they did not break.

Dropsy: Into a half-gallon of cider, put one handful of crushed parsley, a handful of crushed horseradish, and a tablespoonful of juniper berries. After letting the mixture stand for twenty-four hours in a warm place, take half a tumblerful before each meal.

Dysentery: Gather the green leaves of the sunflower and dry and steep into a tea. Drink the tea, but give sparingly to babies.

Earache: Pour into the aching ear a couple of drops of warm oil, then plug the ear with cotton and apply a warm cloth; or place the ear at the end of a funnel that has been inverted over a pan of boiling water and allow the steam to penetrate; or take live coals and sprinkle generously with sugar, and hold the ear to the vapor.

Easy childbirth: Three months before delivery, take as a tea each night a good drink of the following: a tablespoon of flaxseed and another of slippery elm in a gallon of boiling water.

Eczema: Indians made a salve of ant eggs, and it is said that the acid in the eggs was effective. A white remedy: boil together a pint of pine tar and another of thick cream until only one pint remains. Spread this mixture over the body, put on heavy underwear, and keep it on for three weeks, and then remove and bathe. This remedy is said to be unfailing.

Emetic: Tea made from the bark of a peach tree.

Felon: Scrape common laundry soap and mix into it turpentine to make a salve.

Fever: Sagebrush tea is said to be excellent in the treatment of Rocky Mountain (tick) fever. It is a bitter brew to take, and possibly a part of its potency lies in the horrible taste.

Flu: Mix vinegar, butter, sugar, water, and red pepper in a hot solution and drink copiously. The proportion of the ingredients seems not to matter.

Freckles: To remove freckles, moisten a chunk of saltpeter and rub the freckles daily; or give the face or other affected parts a good bath in ripe strawberries before going to bed. To clear the skin, drink milk in which you have boiled buckshot.

Headache: Apply a mustard plaster to the pit of the stomach.

Hiccough: If holding your breath until you count to fifty does not work, saturate a lump of sugar in vinegar and eat slowly, or take a fizz drink of vinegar and soda.

Inflammation: Apply a poultice of melted sugar and soap, or of plain axle grease. The latter was a common remedy in early times.

Ingrown toenail: Cut a V on the center edge of the nail and keep the nail scraped thin.

Insanity: The only remedy reported is generous application of hot mustard to the stomach and loins.

Itch: Apply a salve made of equal parts of mustard and lard.

Lameness: From the Raft River country comes the statement: There ain't nuthun better to cure lameness than sheep manure in hot water. (Applied externally, of course.)

Measles: From the same country, according to Annie Pike Greenwood: Now, fer to bring out the measles when they have went in on your child, you jest give it a tea made out of chicken manure. It sure brings out the measles.

Mumps: Put a bowl of bread crumbs in a pan of warm milk, and then of the mixture make a poultice between cotton towels and apply to the face. It was commonly believed, of course, that a silk string around the neck would keep the mumps from going down.

Neuralgia: Soak a woolen rag in vinegar, heat a flat iron enough to cause a vapor, place the rag over the affected part and apply the iron to the rag. Repeat frequently. The *Idaho World* reported for Oct. 17, 1879: Several evenings ago, says W. H. of our city, I was attacked with a severe dental neuralgia. After resorting to friction, cold and hot applications, without obtaining relief, I lay on my bed trusting that sleep might come. But the excruciating pain continued and while I was suffering the tortures of the double damned, undecided whether to arouse the druggist or chop my head off, I bethought me of what I had read of an anaesthetic which always we carry with us. Thereupon I began to inflate my lungs to their utmost capacity, then to exhale. Immediately the pain began to lessen and after a few repetitions of this, it had entirely ceased, being displaced with a delightful tickling sensation in the gums. In no time at all I was fast asleep.

Nosebleed: If applications of cold water are unavailing, put a wad of paper into the mouth and chew vigorously.

Objects in eye: The common (and it seems almost the only) remedy is flaxseed.

Perspiration: Said the *Idaho World,* Dec. 10, 1864: The unpleasant odor produced by perspiration is frequently the source of vexation to persons subject to it. Nothing is simpler than to remove this odor much more effectively than by the applications of such costly perfumes as are in use. It is only necessary to procure some compound spirits of ammonia and place about two tablespoonsful in a basin of water. Washing the face, arms and hands with this leaves the skin as clean, fresh and sweet as one could wish.

Pimples: To prevent pimples apply a mixture of sulphur and molasses; to bring to a head, cover with mild soap or with the inner skin of a raw egg.

Pneumonia: Mix equal parts of kerosene, turpentine, and lard and rub the chest well and then soak a cloth in the mixture and apply and keep the application warm. A second: boil three large potatoes with their skins on, mash, and add a tablespoon of mustard, another of salt, and a teaspoon of lobelia. Apply the mixture in muslin bags to both the chest and back and change as they cool. A third: kill a chicken and cut it open and use the warm organs as a poultice on the chest. A fourth: make a poultice of ground flaxseed and water and cover with mustard before applying. A fifth: boil together a gallon of vinegar, a package of red pepper, and a handful of salt and apply on a wet towel to the chest and throat. All these preparations should be changed as soon as they have cooled.

Rheumatism: Bandage the swollen part with a red woolen rag; take a lemon every day for three days, miss three days, and repeat until a dozen have been taken; carry a potato in the pocket until it withers; wear a copper bracelet on the wrists and ankles (this is very common in Idaho); or try a Chinese remedy and behead a rattlesnake, put into a jar and cover with rice whisky and leave for a year, then drink the whisky. If all of these fail, make a ring of a horseshoe and wear on your finger. Many old-timers who almost believe that electricity is the substance of life argue that the ring or the copper bracelet draws the juice to the body and circulates it. It seems doubtful, however, if any of these cures are quite so effective as less starch and meats in the diet; but old-timers refuse to listen to such nonsense as diet and scour the country to learn what metal produces the best results as a lightning rod.

Ringworm: Apply a mixture of olive oil and sulphur. "I have seen this remedy used many times and it has always produced results."

Scurvy: Apply uncooked potatoes sliced and soaked in vinegar.

Severe constipation: Cook a package of fine-cut tobacco in a quart of boiling water and strain. Use a pint as an enema, and if necessary repeat with a second pint. This may slightly inebriate but the effect will soon pass.

Smallpox: Take frequent doses of brandy in which salt-peter has been dissolved. The *Boise News* reported June 4, 1865, that thousands of cases had been cured in England with this remedy: cream of tartar, ¾ oz.; rhubarb, 12 grains; cold water, one pint. This dose is from a quarter to half a pint, though a pint may be taken in extreme cases.

Snowblindness: Apply to the eyes a poultice of tea leaves.

Sore throat: Many are the remedies for this ailment, ranging all the way through sense and nonsense. (1) Take a black stocking and turn it wrong side out and tie it around the throat with the heel over the Adam's apple. (2) In a common but clean pipe, smoke equal parts of ground coffee and sawdust of pine. (3) Betty Changnon, of Idaho Falls, says that in early days, her great-grandmother cured sore throat in her grandfather by buttering a small piece of pork and fastening it to a string, thrusting the morsel down her son's throat, and then with the string drawing it up and allowing it to be swallowed and drawn up again, repeating many times. (4) Mix turpentine with sweet oil (or if you have none, with lard) and take internally. (5) Bake onions in sugar until a sirup is formed and take a spoonful at a time: it is said that if the medicine doesn't cure, the odor of it will. (6) Boil white navy beans until soft and make a mash and apply as a poultice. (7) Mix lard and kerosene equally and apply. (8) In early times, frontiersmen doctored with quinine and bitter herbs, and the Indians used powdered sagebrush. After heating flat stones, they placed on them tender fresh leaves and powdered them by rubbing the stones together; whereupon they dusted the powder into the sick throat, or thrust their fingers into the throat after they had been moistened and dipped into the powder.

Stings: To a bee sting apply a poultice of mud.

Stomachache: Drink tea made of ground pumpkin seeds or of alfalfa leaves, or apply cold packs to the stomach.

Sty: The only home remedies reported take some form of rubbing the sty with a potent object, such as a cat's tail or a gold wedding ring.

Teething: Kill a rabbit and put the warm brains in a cloth and rub on the gums while warm; and if that doesn't work, find a child that has never seen its father and persuade him to blow his breath into the mouth of the teething youngster.

Ulcer: For ulcer of the stomach, drink tea made of dry gizzards from chickens, being sure to use the muscular skin.

Warts: Most of the cures for warts are superstitions, though some burn them off with acids or with hot irons, or dig them out and cauterize the wound. If you don't fancy measures so extreme, you may take an old and rusted piece of iron and heat it and plunge it into a pan of cold water, and then bathe your warts, though many applications may be necessary; or apply the milk from healthy stems of milkweed plant; or press the wart against a piece of wood and then burn the wood and mix the ashes with lard to make a salve (some old-timers swear by this remedy); or cut a potato in half and rub on the wart and throw the potato away, provided you do not observe where the potato goes to; or touch the wart with a rock and then place the rock in a paper bag where some unwary simpleton will pick it up and get the wart. This method sounds very un-Christian but seems to have many supporters. Or you may rub your wart with a piece of bacon and then bury it, and rest assured that the wart will disappear before the bacon rots. Or you may rub an ear of corn on the wart until it bleeds and feed the corn to a chicken.

Whooping cough: Gather chestnut leaves just before the nuts fall; boil and strain and sweeten with brown sugar, and take frequent but small doses.

APPENDICES

—❧—

IN TRYING to gather folk songs and idiomatic speech indigenous to Idaho, we encountered the same problems that faced us in such materials as customs and Indian legends. Many songs came in, but few of them had any more to do with Idaho than Idaho has with the banks of the Wabash. Many of them were minor variants of folk songs which originated elsewhere; and a few were sentimental verses that had only local interest if any at all. It is not assumed that most of the songs included here are of folk origin, or that some of them in other variants have not been published before. It seems hardly necessary to point out that the best of the material gathered was too profane or lewd for inclusion.

The same problem was present in regard to speech. Students and others sent in hundreds of idioms, colloquialisms, and sayings; but most of them were contemporary college slang or had become trite through widespread use. In the following lists, some of the vernacular is still in vigorous service; some of it is heard only infrequently even among old-timers; and perhaps a little of it is never heard anywhere within the State, though records declare its existence a half-century or more ago.

Cowboy's Square Dance

Git yer little sagehens ready:
Trot 'em out upon the floor—
Line up there, you cusses! Steady!
Lively, now! One couple more.
Shorty, shed that ol' sombrero.
Broncho, douse that cigarette.
Stop yer cussin' Casimero,
'Fore the ladies! Now all set.

S'lute yer ladies, all together,
Ladies opposite the same;
Hit the lumber with yer leather!
Balance all, an' swing yer dame!
Bunch the heifers in the middle!
Circle stags, an' do-so-do—
Pay attention to the fiddle!
Swing her 'round an' off you go!

First four forward! Back to places!
Second feller! Shuffle back!
Now you got it down to cases,
Swing 'em till their trotters crack!
Gents all right a heel an' toein'.
Swing 'em! Kiss 'em if you kin!
On to the next, an' keep a-goin'
Till you hit yer pards agin!

Gents to center; ladies 'round 'em
Form a basket: balance all.
Whirl yer gals to where you found 'em,
Promenade around the hall!
Balance to yer pards, an' trot 'em
'Round the circle double quick!
Grab an' kiss 'em while you've got 'em!
Hold 'em to it if they kick!

Ladies left hand to yer sonnies!
Alaman! Grand right an' left!
Balance all an' swing yer honies—
Pick 'em up and feel their heft!
Promenade like skeery cattle!
Balance all an' swing yer sweets!
Shake yer spurs an' make 'em rattle!
Keno! Promenade to seats!

Waltz Quadrille

First couple down center,
And there you divide;
Ladies to the right,
And gents to the left side.

Honor your partner,
And don't be afraid:
Swing on the corner
With a waltz promenade.

(Repeat—second, third, and fourth couples.)

Dance Calls[1]

Oh, now to give the right hand across
And take that step in time;
Now hold your grip with the left hand back
And balance four in a line.

Break in the center and swing half round
And balance there again.
Now break and swing with your partner home
And the same two ladies change;
Change right back with a half promenade
And a half right and left.

Then through to the next lady doseedoe
And the gent you know.
Break with the right and swing with the left.
Right hand to your partner and through to the next.

---

1 From the Grangeville area.

Now the right hand across as in the first verse;
When the four couples have joined in then
A left alleman and a left alleman
And why in the world don't you right and left grand?

Meet your partner with a double elbow
And keep a hooking on as around you go;
Then promenade there—you know where—
And I don't care.

Quadrille[1]

Hands in your pockets,
And backs to the wall:
Chew your tobacco,
And balance all.
        Alaman left!
Everybody swing:
Promenade the ring.
First couple lead out to the right
Four hands across.
Ladies bow,
The gents know how.
Swing 'em once and a half
Right and left through,
On to the next,
And four hands across.
The ladies bow,
The gents come under,
And swing like thunder:
Break and through
And on to the next.
The ladies bow:
The gents be quick
And swing like heck—
And right and left through
And home again
With a grand right and left
And promenade all!

(Second, third, and fourth couples repeat.)

---

1 *Idem.*

Ida Ho

For her I'd leave Virginia,
I'd leave my Mary Land.
I'd part with Mrs. Sippi,
That widow, fair and bland.

I'd leave Louisa Anna,
And other Annas, too.
I'd bid farewell to Georgia,
Though Georgia would be true.

I'd part with Minna Sota;
I'd part with Della Ware.
I'd leave brunette Miss Souri,
Or the Carolina pair.

These women are all lovely,
True-hearted girls, I know;
But I'd give them all the go-by
And stick to Ida Ho.

I like her breezy manners;
I like her honest ways;
I like her in the moonlight,
And in the sunny days.

Goodbye, my own Virginia,
And other girls I know;
I'm hanging around the gatepost
Of a girl named Ida Ho!

Fallen Leaf

Far beyond the rolling prairies where the noble forest lies,
Lived the fairest Indian maiden ever seen by mortal eyes.
She whose eyes were like the moonbeams, daughter of a
　　　warrior chief,
Sought to cheer our homes in autumn, and they called her
　　　Fallen Leaf.

Chorus

Fallen Leaf, the breezes whispered of thy spirit's early flight,
And within our lonely wigwam there's a wail of woe tonight.

From the depth of lonely forest all alone one summer day
Came a stranger lame and weary from a long and lonesome
way.
Weeks passed by, but still he lingered; gently, "Fallen Leaf!"
he cried,
And with a smile of love she promised soon to be his wood-
land bride.

Chorus

Late one summer day he wandered 'cross the prairie wastes
alone;
Long she watched and long she waited, but his fate was
never known.
With the summer leaves she faded, with the autumn leaves
she died;
And we closed her eyes in slumber by the Salmon River side.

Chorus

The End of Louie Malone

Louie Malone yelled, "Reach for the sky!"
But the guard on the stagecoach was young and spry.
A kick of his boot, a flick of his wrist,
And Louie, the bandit, fired and missed.
The guard dropped his shotgun, whipped out his Colts,
And they blasted at Louie like twin thunderbolts.

Louie was a robber, robbed all alone,
And now things were hot for the son of Malone.
The slugs buzzed around him like bees in a swarm,
And for seconds the fighting was getting right warm.
When the smoke cleared away, Louie was found
In a puddle of red lying then on the ground.
The guard wasn't nicked, and it's just to say
That you can't get away with it: crime doesn't pay.

The End of
Louie Malone

Eagle Rock[1]

Millionaires grow in Chicago
In mansions of marble and pride;
Homes grow in Eagle Rock,
And friendships, true and tried.

Plutocracy thrives in proud New York
Though poverty dogs its heel;
Real brotherhood grows on Eagle Rock,
Where hearts have time to feel.

It's pleasant to play in Paris
Where gaiety gains renown;
But oh! when it comes to living
Give me that dear Idaho town.

Curly Joe

A mile below Blue Canyon,
On the lonely Pinion trail,
Near the little town of Sanctos,
Nestled in a quiet dale,
Is the grave of a young cowboy,
Whose name is now unknown,
Save by a few frontiersmen
Who call the spot their own.

He was as fine a rider
As ever forked a steed;
He was brave and kind and generous,
Never did a dirty deed.
Curly Joe's the name he went by—
'Twas enough, none cared to know
If he ever had another,
So they called him Curly Joe.

'Bout a mile from the Sanctos village
Lived an ex-grandee of Spain,
And his daughter, Bonnie Enza,
Called the White Rose of the Plain.

---

1 The early name of Idaho Falls.

Curly loved this high-born lassie,
Since that time so long ago
When he found her on the mountains
Lost and blinded by the snow.

But coquettish was fair Enza,
'Tis a woman's foolish trait,
That has blasted many a manhood
Like the harsh decrees of fate;
When pressed in earnest language,
Not flowery but sincere,
For an answer to his question
She smiled and shed a tear.

When she answered, "Really, Joe Boy,
Quite wearisome you grow.
Your sister, Sir, forever,
But your wife, no never, Joe."
Not another word was spoken;
In a week poor Joe was dead,
Killed by a bucking broncho,
Or at least that's what they said.

For many a year the tombstone
That marked this cowboy's grave
In quaint and curious language
This prophetic warning gave:
"Never hope to win the daughter
Of the boss that owns the brand,
For I tried it and changed ranges
To a far and better land."

Idaho's Yankee Doodle

Oh! where's that Yankee Doodle, Dandy?
You've heard of him in days of yore.
The girls would give him nuts and candy
To pose for them by their front door.

CHORUS

Oh! Yankee Doodle, Doodle, Dandy,
Wherever you may chance to roam,
Just keep your mind on nuts and candy
And all the girls 'way back home.

Clawhammer coat and striped trousers,
A hat that reached high in the air,
A mongrel dog whose name was Towser
That followed him most everywhere.

CHORUS

He once did ride upon a pony
Wherever he was wont to go.
He once was fed on macaroni
But now he lives upon black crow.

CHORUS

He's now dressed up in rags and tatters
Because the times, they are so hard.
His hat has been sent off to the hatter's
Or pawned to buy some bread and lard.

CHORUS

Farewell to Old Elm[1]

Farewell to old Elm,
I can no longer stay.
Hard times and relations
Have driven me away.
Hard times and the rangers
Have caused me to roam;
I am a southern cowboy
And Elm is my home.

I have some friends on Elm Creek,
I love the tracks they make;
And when I get to Idaho
I hope to make a stake.

---

1 An old cowboy song sent in by Mrs. Adee Hawes of Bruneau.

And if I do they'd never see
The kindness they have done;
It's when I lived on Elm
And when I had to run.

The officers are no gentlemen,
They haven't got any soul;
They drove me from my fireside,
They drove me out in the cold;
Till I am so tired,
That I can hardly go to Idaho.

The sheriff is no gentleman,
He is nothing but a hog:
He thought he'd catch John Shackleford,
He'd catch him with his dogs.
With his dogs and horse
He'd thought he'd run him down,
And treat him like his brother
Who now lies in the ground.

John Shackleford, a gentleman
Perhaps you do not know.
He mounts his Halama charger
And a ranging he does go!
The sheriff went out scouting
Down on the Wilson ranch,
Where Lige was hung for robbing
Down on the hobble branch.

I hope I've done no injury
In the country where I stayed.
I know I rode stray horses
And one that was a gray.
But riding stray horses
That's the worst I ever done;
And that is no occasion
For me to have to run.

Now when this war is over
And I return again,
If I am not mighty mistaken
Some one will hunt a limb.

Now when this war is over
And I return again,
I think we'll have a reckoning
And see who was to blame.

Crossing the Plains[1]

I will sing you a song, it may be a sad one,
Of trials and troubles and when they first begun.
I left my kind friends and kindred at home
And left for the coulees and mountains to roam.

You've heard tell of those wild Sioux out on the plains
A-killing some drivers and robbing their trains,
A-killing some drivers with their arrows and bows;
When captured by Indians, no mercy they showed.

We traveled along till we came to the flat
And we pitched up our tents on the edge of that;
We spread out our blankets on green grassy ground
Where our mules and horses were feeding around.

Just sat there a moment; we heard a loud yell
And a band of Sioux Indians dashed into our dell.
We sprang to our rifles with blood in our eye,
"Come all of you, comrades, let us fight till we die."

They made a bold dash and came after our train.
The arrows flew around us like hail and like rain!
I saw the red chief lying dead in his gore.
They whooped and they yelled and we saw them no more.

We hitched up our horses and started again,
But more bloody battles we had on the plain.
And in our last battle our two brave boys fell.
And we laid them to rest in the green grassy dell.

---

1 This was sung in Idaho sixty years ago.

The Indian Lass[1]

As I was strolling for pleasure one day
In deep meditation with care cast away;
As I was strolling along on the grass,
Who should I meet but a fair Indian lass?

She knelt down beside me, took hold of my hand;
Said, "You're a stranger, not one of our kind.
But if you will follow you are welcome to come
To my little home in a wild wood grove."

This fair little lass was smartest of her kind;
She taught me a part of her own heart's design.
Although I was a stranger she took me into her home.
I will remember that lass wherever I roam.

'Twas early one morn, at the dawn of the day,
This fair little lass heard myself say,
"I'm going to leave you, I am going today,
My ship is out there and away I will steer."

The last time I saw her was down on the sand.
The ship was a-passing, she was waving her hand,
Saying, "When you get home, to the ones that you love,
Will you think of the lass in the wild willow grove?"

Now I am at home, on my own native shore,
Where friends and relatives greet me once more;
But of all that's around me not one do I see,
Not one that's as kind as the lass o'er the sea.

Kamiah Springs[2]

'Twas the summer of 1879.
As a young man in my prime,
I drove my stock to Washington
Across the Oregon line.

---

1 This was sung on the ranges a half-century ago.
2 A ballad written around the Indian fight at Kamiah Springs, Oct. 22, 1879.

We started from big Buttercreek,
My friend, Job Smith, an' I,
An' we found the stockman's paradise
Where the bunch-grass grew waist-high.

An' our hearts were light an' happy;
Till one October night
The Injuns swooped down on us,
An' we had that awful fight.

An Injun held me by the hair;
His knife was raised on high;
A shot rang out from Job Smith's gun,
An' an Injun fell to die.

Quick as a cat, I leaped for guns;
A pair of Colts had I.
The moon was shining brightly,
An' Indians fell close by.

Two score years have passed an' gone
Since that bright October night.
My friend, Job Smith, is sleeping now;
I live to tell the fight.

But now I'm old an' feeble,
An' my days are nearly o'er.
Job, have my cayuse saddled
When we meet on yon bright shore.

They may have their choo-choo wagons there;
Likewise, their aeroplanes,
But I'll take the deck of a cayuse,
An' ride the western range.

Verse of a Pioneer Song[1]

My mother and father were very poor people;
They lived by a church which had a high steeple.
They raised apples but sold them so low
They made no fortune in Idaho.

---

1 This verse is from a song which used to be popular in pioneer times in southwestern Idaho.

Mochyn Dee[1]

All you people come and listen;
Tear-drops in your eyes will glisten;
Pain your hearts will now be rending
At our Mochyn's sudden ending!

CHORUS

O! how sad indeed are we!
O! how sad indeed are we!
There was grief and tribulation
When we lost the Mochyn Dee!

What did cause the termination
Of our Mochyn's pilgrimation?
Was it too much wash or barley
That did waft her home so early?

CHORUS

Yes, the truth we must be telling:
Too much grain her stomach swelling
She got very ill and poorly—
Closed her eyes and went to glory!

CHORUS

Quickly Dai ran to Llwyncelyn,
Fetching Matty to the Mochyn.
Matty said, to our horror,
That the pig would not recover!

CHORUS

Then we bought a polished coffin—
Silver knobs and velvet trimming;
And a vault of bricks and mortar
In the church-yard we did order.

CHORUS

---

1 From the Malad Valley.

Then we sent to Isaac Thomas
For his hearse which is so famous,
And for horses black as mourning
For to drive our poor old Mochyn!

CHORUS

Then the reverend Thomas Griffiths
Came to read the funeral service.
All the people there were sobbing
At the funeral of the Mochyn!

CHORUS

Mary Jones and Peggy Williams
Led the way in solemn silence.
All the people in the county
At the grave were weeping plenty.

CHORUS

Then we went home nice and tidy,
For one heart was very heavy.
But the girls were crying shocking—
'Cause they'd gone and lost the Mochyn!

CHORUS

Then we looked with painful feeling
At the hooks upon the ceiling
Not a single side of bacon!—
'Twas a loss to lose the Mochyn!

CHORUS

Very nice to have for dinner
Is some bacon and patater.
Now, alas! we have to want it
For our Mochyn's kicked the bucket!

CHORUS

Now, my friends, my song is ended;
Note the warning I've intended;
Mind to act with great discretion
When you go to feed your Mochyn!

The White Captive[1]

The sun had gone down on the hills in the west,
The last beams had faded on the massive hill crest,
Amid beauties of nature and charms of the fair,
Amanda lay bound, with her white neck all bare.

At the foot of the mountains where Amanda doth sigh
At the hoot of the owl or the catamount's cry
Or the howl of the wolf in some low ground swell,
Like the sound of a dead-fall or a tree when it fell,

The watch fire was kindled, 'twas fanned by a breeze
And the red embers shone on the evergreen trees;
And fierce was the look of the wild savages seen
Impatient to join in their war dancing song.

Then in was brought the captive, all friendless forlorn,
Her face bathed in blood, her garments all torn.
She swore vengeance in the face of her foes,
Gave a sigh for the time when her sufferings might close.

Young Albion, the chief of the warriors, drew near,
He'd an eye like an eagle and a step like a deer,
And a heart that would scorn her freedom to save,
Gave a sigh for her suffering and an eye for her grave.

"Forbear," says young Albion, "your torture forbear.
This damsel shall live, by the Great Father I swear.
This night if a victim must burn at your tree,
Young Albion, your leader, the victim shall be."

At the dusk of evening and close of day,
A birch bark canoe was seen gliding away.
As swift as the wild duck that glides by their side,
Young Albion and Amanda together doth ride.

---

1 This song was popular sixty years ago.

In the dawn of the morning a white cot was seen
Amid blue curling smoke and wild willows green;
And great was her joy when she came to that shore
To see her old father and mother once more.

Young Albion stood by and saw them embrace.
His heart overjoyed, tears ran down his face,
And all that he asked for was kindness and food
From the father of Amanda to the Chief of the Wood.

The Trail to Idaho

I made up my mind to change my way,
And quit my crowd that was so gay;
I left my darling girl behind,
She said her heart was only mine.

It was in the year of eighty-three
That a cattleman hired me.
He says, "Young feller, I want you to go
And drive the herd into Idaho."

When I arrived at the once-loved home
I called for the darling of my own.
They said she had married a richer life,
Therefore, wild cowboy, seek another wife.

"Oh! Buddie, Oh! Buddie, please stay at home,
Don't be forever on the roam.
There is many a girl more true than I
So, pray don't go where the bullets fly."

"It's curse your gold and your silver, too;
God pity a girl that won't prove true!
I'll travel West where the bullets fly.
I'll stay on the trail until I die."

Idaho Speech

As big as a skinned ox—usually applied to persons.

As low as a hog's belly—depressed; down at the mouth.

Bob-wire—barbed wire.

Brush-whip—to rebuke mildly.

Busier than Hattie's flea—extremely busy.

Catty-cornered—cater-cornered.

Chin-music—incessant (and usually empty) talk.

Clear-grit—the genuine article.

Cut of your jib—a contemptuous appraisal of character or personality.

Doodlebug—unscrupulous mine promoter.

Doughgod—a chunk of (usually) baking-powder bread.

Fat as a hen's forehead—meager.

Give it a lick and a promise—to do carelessly.

Gunsight lode—an ore lode found and then lost.

Hairow—horror.

Hell beating tanbark—hasten; to go in a hurry.

Hightailing—to go swiftly. The expression comes from the fact that horses raise their tails high fleeing.

Hit the high lonesome—to depart, usually in haste; or to set out for an unknown destination.

In spite of hell and high water—in spite of all obstacles.

In the lurks—in the lurch.

Knight of the road—stagecoach robber.

Made the riffle—was successful.

Make a poor mouth—plead poverty.

Mormon candy—raw carrot.

Mormon rain—a dust storm.

Mouth-almighty—boastful.

Not on your tintype—emphatic refusal.

Ragtag and bobtail—odds and ends.

Rig—wagon or other vehicle.

Rig out—to prepare, usually for a journey.

Ring-boned, knock-kneed, and spavined—an expression of contempt or uselessness.

Scringe—to cringe.

Slept on a buffalo robe—slept on the earth.

Sourdough—old-timer.

Spell—a short period of time; to spell equals to change off, to take turns with a person laboring; or to spell a beast laboring, meaning to allow it to rest.

Stand up to the rock—face the situation.

Starkled—startled.

Stick a pin there—make a note of it.

Summer foller—summer fallow.

Sweethearten a girl—to woo.

Swivel—shrivel.

They fit—they fought.

Till hell wouldn't have it—the expression may mean thoroughly used up; or beaten or vanquished.

To goak—to goad.

To fork—to mount (usually) a horse: "He forked his horse."

To heft—to estimate weight of by lifting.

To kick the wind—to cut capers.

To light and set—to dismount and talk awhile.

To lallygag—to flirt.

Tough it out—endure.

Vent the brand—change ownership.

Whip the devil around the stump—to indulge in self-excuses.

Whitetop—a buggy.

Some Mild Profanity

By the bald-headed Jews—the more emphatic variants substitute, of course, members of the Trinity.

Dod rabbit it!—this is not common, and seems to be mild.

*A flea-bitten son-of-a——*flea-bitten has variants.

Hellfire and brimstone!—often an exclamation of surprise or (more commonly) disgust.

The hell you bawl out!—this seems not to be common.

Holy jumped-up Moses!—Moses often yields to members of the Trinity.

Jumpun blue blazes!—a meaningless expletive.

Leapun lizards!—much like jumpun blue blazes.

My holy sainted aunt!—though declared to be not modern, this savors of college slang.

"Them's the by Goddest horses that ever be damned!"—reported from the Salmon River country.

Picturesque Expressions

The sky looks like it's making big for a storm.

A miner said of a good-for-nothing acquaintance: "I panned him clean down to bedrock but I couldn't raise a color."

An old German in the Grangeville area owned a horse that was injured; and when asked how it had happened he said: "Oh, he yust tied himself loose and kicked himself mit anoder horse." This explanation has been applied to various situations and is still heard around campfires.

An Idaho native was heard to say: "Damn it, this coffee is strong enough to float an iron wedge around Cape Horn!"

Before the railroad came to Lewiston, it was customary to say of a person going to Portland that he "is going below" and of one going to Mount Idaho that "he is going above."

These were common expressions many years ago: Die dog or eat the hatchet; land a Goshen!; cripes Maria; you're as crazy as a bay steer in a cornfield.

Jargon

The following is mining jargon in the Pierce City area:

The break-up—spring.

Clean-up—mineral taken from a sluice-box.

Diggins—a mine.

Palouser—a lard pail and candle converted into a lantern.

Mud stick—a shovel.

Quick—mercury.

Strip—to remove the top earth.

Salt—to salt is to place gold on a worthless prospect to deceive the unwary into investing. The deception is still practiced.

The following is lumberjack jargon in the St. Maries area and elsewhere:

Brush ape—one who clears away brush.

Bull of the woods—the foreman.

Gut robber—the cook.

Punk—bread.

Put her in the gippo notch—to labor very hard.

Road monkey—a laborer on the road.

School mom—a tree that forks; forked pole used in loading.

Skybound—a tree hard to fell.

Sweat pads—hot cakes.

Tail down—to roll a log onto a skidway.

Widow-maker—a falling tree top or branch.

Wrap her up—to quit a job.

The following is reported as the speech of a lumberjack who was injured and taken to a hospital. When asked how it happened, he said: A bundle-stiff (itinerant worker) wheeled in over the road and hit the push-up (foreman) for a job. He put him to work sky-hooking (top-loading) with me, but seeing he was a stubble-jumper (greenhorn), the school mom (forked pole used in loading) gunned (turned) and got me.

The following is reported as the talk of a southwest Idaho cowboy: In the mornun the night-herder rolls out of his soogan (bed-roll) and rolls a quirlie (cigarette). Jist about when the hand is chasun after a cavvy (horse herd), the coolie yells beans, and the cowboys fall in line to grab their shoe soles (pancakes) and snowballs (biscuits) and sheep-dip (coffee). Then each man gits his own broomtail (pony) and drags out (loads) a top horse (his favorite horse). Then he throws on the kak (saddle) and screws hisself on tight (assumes a firm position) and tops him off (lets the horse go). The old bronc might crow hop (jump in a straight line) or unwind (twist and turn).

The following is railroad jargon in the Pocatello area:

The big nuts—superintendent.

The brains—train dispatcher.

Brass buttons—passenger crews.

Car toad—car inspector.

Chain gang—freight men.

The drag—train with dead freight.

Grabber—conductor.

The ham—telegraph operator.

The highball—proceed signal.

Hog head—engineer.

Manifests—fast freights.

Rattler—freight train.

The redball—train with perishables.

Riding the plush—riding a passenger train.

Sailers—streamliners.

Section jerry—section hand.

Shack; or *the rail*—brakeman.

The snake—switchman.

The tallowpot—fireman.

To pull the pin—to resign.

Varnished cars—passenger train.

The washout—stop signal.

INDEX

꒜